The Search for a Christian Education —
Since 1940

BOOKS BY KENDIG BRUBAKER CULLY
Published by The Westminster Press®

The Search for a Christian Education —
Since 1940

The Westminster Dictionary
of Christian Education (ed.)

Basic Writings
in Christian Education (ed.)

Prayers for Church Workers (ed.)

BOOKS BY KENDIG B. CULLY AND IRIS V. CULLY
Published by The Westminster Press®

An Introductory Theological Wordbook

The Search for a Christian Education— Since 1940

by

KENDIG BRUBAKER CULLY

THE WESTMINSTER PRESS

Philadelphia

Published by The Westminster Press®
Philadelphia, Pennsylvania

PRINTED IN THE UNITED STATES OF AMERICA

To

A. J. WILLIAM MYERS,
who has embodied in his life
and teaching all that the liberal
spirit connotes

Contents

Preface

A VERITABLE revolution has taken place in the field of religious education since about 1940. This revolution has been more pronounced in the theoretical than in the practical aspects of the church's educational work. To be sure, there have been exciting curricular developments and some fairly new methodological efforts; but to the extent to which these have developed, they are reflections of the changed orientation on the intellectual level. Back of any structure is the ideology on which it rests. The purpose of the present book is to examine the various forms that this intellectual revamping of religious education has taken, and to classify, insofar as possible, the distinctive contributions of several schools of thought within the Christian community as it manifests the educational effort. Finally, some attempt will be made to generalize a measure of the matter that has constituted the principal concern of the study, and to set forth an argument for deeper historical foundations for Christian education, both as a discipline and as a work of the church.

My original intent was to call this book something like " The Churches in Search of an Education." The plural " churches " did not please me greatly, let me freely admit,

because of a predisposition to want to think in terms of the
one body of Christ. (The ecumenical education of our day
has thus conditioned the view of one Christian, so that he
has some guilt feelings even about suggesting the possibility of a plurality of bodies bearing the name of Jesus
Christ!) Yet, to be realistic about it, it did seem that there
was not strong evidence to the effect that one church was
in fact available to essay the educational task, in spite of
all the agencies that have worked toward that end for so
long. Furthermore, it seemed evident that although the
churches, through organized media such as the Division of
Christian Education of the National Council of the
Churches of Christ in the U.S.A., had done a great deal to
prepare statements of goals and to issue outlines for joint
curricular efforts, actually such statements and curricula
could scarcely be claimed as speaking for all Christendom.[1] Even more basic, however, was the realization that
all the branches of the Christian church actually reflected
in their educational choices ideas that first emanated from
individual theoreticians (though the use thereof certainly
was not narrowly restricted to writers from particular confessional circles). Hence the present title, THE SEARCH FOR
A CHRISTIAN EDUCATION, arose in my mind in place of the
earlier one, which now, except for its possibly felicitous
echo of Luigi Pirandello's *Six Characters in Search of an
Author,* seems to have little other merit!

I should like to express my appreciation to students in
seminars during the last decade or more in the schools
where I have offered courses, variously entitled " Theology
and Christian Education," " Theological Foundations of
Christian Education," or " Philosophies of Religious Education." Such seminars have been offered at Seabury-
Western Theological Seminary and The Biblical Seminary

in New York, in connection with full-time professorial teaching; and in the following schools, where I have been privileged to serve as guest professor, either in the regular academic year or in summer sessions: Bethany Theological Seminary, Lutheran School of Theology (Chicago), Pacific School of Religion, Union Theological Seminary (New York), and the University of Pittsburgh. In all these places mine has been the typical professor's experience of the teacher's being taught much by his students.

Most of the actual writing of this book was done during the summer of 1964 at Pittsburgh. I want especially to thank Prof. Lawrence C. Little, of the University of Pittsburgh, for inviting me to take on some of his interesting and stimulating students for six weeks, and Dr. William Bradbury, rector of the Church of the Ascension (Protestant Episcopal), for letting me use a comfortable office off the sacristy while I filled in for him at services and otherwise kept busy with the typewriter.

My wife, Iris V. Cully, has been a most helpful consultant as the chapters have evolved. Since she is herself the subject of a part of one chapter, I must hasten to say that she was not invited to " screen " that section. Nor can I " blame " her, either, for the conclusions in any of the chapters!

K. B. C.

New York City

1

A Question and a Challenge

THOSE who were studying in theological schools during the 1930's were living in a theological climate that, in retrospect, seems almost antediluvian. Except for a few avant-garde figures like Reinhold Niebuhr at Union Theological Seminary, New York, and Edwin Lewis at Drew Theological Seminary, the leading interdenominational chairs in such places as New Haven, Hartford, Chicago, and Berkeley were occupied by exponents of the traditional liberalist positions. Denominational seminaries from Boston to San Francisco and everywhere in between had much the same orientation, save for the distinctive flavors educed from their respective confessional traditions.

The religious education movement, which had been riding on top of the waves during the 1920's, was beginning to run into shoals as the decade proceeded. When the economic depression came along, one immediate effect was to destroy any semblance of security that directors of religious education, trained in the various schools set up for this new profession, may have thought to have achieved. Little did the graduates of the previous two decades know that the intellectual foundations on which their nascent profession had been launched also would soon collapse, or at least become considerably modified.

It is sobering to this writer to recall that he took his divinity degree in the year that the first Kierkegaard translations into English emerged from Walter Lowrie's study. World War II was not even dreamed of as we talked with German exchange students about the differences in ethos between German and American theology. They were usually too absorrbed in mastering spoken English to be able to help us much with an evaluation of the strange new thought world of Karl Barth and others. Of these Continental theologians we heard little from the older professors, and the young instructors' inklings were softly spoken lest they should upset too much the senior faculty upon whose evaluations of their points of view academic futures usually hung. A few who did speak out were rusticated.

In religious education per se, those of us who were doing professional graduate study in that field found that we were being nurtured in a viewpoint that no one seriously questioned. To many religious educators, "theology" was a bit of a nasty word. We seldom asked what were the theological presuppositions underlying such and such an educational approach. "Philosophical" was the preferred term. It was universally assumed that John Dewey had caused the only real methodological breakthrough since Pestalozzi and Froebel. Was not the Progressive Education Association still very much alive? Salvation by education was still assumed to be a proper way to think of the Christian contribution to the world, and democracy was almost a synonym for Christianity. Professors still looked ahead to the kind of world order we should be able to construct cooperatively, and progress was construed as a kind of divine principle.

If these were characteristic notes of the theological seminary communities, the same were even more pronounced in parishes across the land where the people dwelt and worked. If echoes of strident new European voices did occasionally penetrate academic halls, certainly they practically never found their way into the pulpits and thence to the pews. To be sure, there was ample devotional life in evidence, sometimes colored by the kind of strife Harry Emerson Fosdick had been forced to engage in during his notable emergence as the principal preaching voice of Protestant liberalism. Likewise, there was plenty of unexamined Biblical fundamentalism in the air, along with the rationalist " orthodoxy " that had led J. Gresham Machen, of Princeton Theological Seminary, and likeminded colleagues into the formation of a new theological seminary.

The major denominations, however, were quite similarly oriented, educationally speaking, with regard to the theological presuppositions which, though seldom labeled that, were nevertheless strongly in the background. Back of the practical curriculum-making of any given period are always some seminal minds who point out directions, provide the motivating ideas, and become, in effect, the architects of the pedagogical means by which the churches propagate the faith, as they understand it, generation to generation.

Prior to 1940 the pivotal names included such persons as: William Clayton Bower, George Herbert Betts, George Albert Coe, Henry F. Cope, Hugh Hartshorne, A. J. William Myers, Theodore G. Soares, and, of course, overtowering all (though personally quite divorced from any direct involvement with the life of any church) John Dewey. No ecumenical movement, in the sense in which that term has emerged during the last three decades, existed to provide intra-ecclesiastical and interdenominational conversations, but somehow the religious education people had always managed to get together in consensus under their own specialized auspices, as in The Religious Education Association (founded in 1903). It is noteworthy that Prof. Paul H. Vieth's famous study, *The Objectives of Religious Education,* was published as long ago as 1930. That the movement into new directions after 1940 was not wholly or at all a matter of " angry young men " or some other educationally revolutionary group within the church is evidenced by the fact that Professor Vieth himself went right along with the reevaluations he saw were necessary and inevitable in view of the changing theological climate and the world's *Sitz im Leben.* In 1947, under his editorship appeared the distinguished report of the International Council of Religious Education on the nature, aims, and scope of *Christian* (note the change of designation which hereafter was being deemed as more desirable) education entitled *The Church and Christian Education.*[1]

But not everyone in the older, higher echelon of leadership of the religious education movement was willing to go along with these reevaluative steps. Notably, George Albert Coe in his later years was to write somewhat bitterly about the " return " to theology that was becoming characteristic of the younger leaders of the church's educational mission, and the journal *Religious Education* was to see such laments interspersed among articles representing the changing stance. As recently as 1960, William Clayton Bower concurred in my diagnosis that a new climate of opinion had emerged, but insisted that " by no means have all in Israel ' bowed the knee to Baal.' "[2]

THE QUESTION: *Harrison S. Elliott*

Looking back at the reasons for changes of opinion away from the liberalism of pre-1940, we can pinpoint a significant event. That was the publication in 1940 of Harrison S. Elliott's *Can Religious Education Be Christian?* By the time this book was published, Professor Elliott had been established for many years as an important figure in religious education, teaching at Union Theological Seminary, New York, and serving actively in the leadership of The Religious Education Association. This volume represented his doctoral dissertation at Yale University, rewritten for publication.

Here is the problem addressed by Harrison Elliott:

There has been an increasing tendency in the Protestant churches to return to the historical formulations of the Christian religion and to repudiate the adjustments which had been made under the influence of modern scientific and social developments. Instead of being called the savior of the churches, as religious education was previously designated by many, the developments of modern religious education are often attacked as a menace to the churches and an evidence of secularization.[3]

He recognizes the difference between the neoorthodox and fundamentalist types of interpretation, admitting that with neoorthodoxy some new factors had begun to enter the situation. It must be remembered that even though neoorthodoxy had not as yet become dominant or even strong in any American church, Elliott would have been occupying at that time the best possible front-row seat in which to participate in its emergence into conversation, for he was a faculty colleague of Reinhold Niebuhr's at Union! The old battles of the Fosdick variety against fundamentalism of the Biblical inerrancy type were now rather clearly ended in well-defined limits. But neoorthodoxy (which we shall be addressing more fully in Chapter 5) now constituted a different kind of threat to the well-entrenched liberalism that had been expressing itself for some years in experience-centered types of religious nurture. The neoorthodox, Elliott says, recognize modern knowledge, sometimes even espousing a rather radical type of Biblical criticism. "But they emphasize the lack of pertinence of such developments [as scientific, social, and political movements] to Christian faith and experience. Since Christianity is a revealed religion, for them it does not depend upon human knowledge or human processes."[4] Therefore, the issues are quite different and much more subtle than those which had produced conflicts when liberalism was battling evangelistic fundamentalism.

Professor Elliott sought to answer his own question, as raised in the title of his book, concluding that religious education *can* be Christian, but only in the terms in which he himself defined Christianity. After having made an honest effort to analyze the neoorthodox allegations as to the nature of the Christian faith, he rejects them, on the ground that they represent an inadequate Christian understanding.

The issues in regard to religious education center in the source of authority. Those with an authoritarian approach seek to find authority for their interpretations outside of human responsibility in some direct revelation of God. Those with an educational approach recognize that while God has not left himself without witness, man has not been given any direct revelation of the meaning of those manifestations. He has been left to discover these manifestations and to make his own interpretations of them.[5]

In other words, he believes that to be Christian, religious education must rest itself squarely upon experiential grounds, for "there is no one true interpretation of the Christian religion which it is its function to transmit. Rather, religious education is an enterprise in which historical experiences and conceptions are utilized in a process by which individuals and groups come to experiences and convictions which are meaningful for them today." [6]

In a sense, Elliott seems to be saying, God chooses to reveal himself through the educational process itself. "It is only through such a process that God becomes known or that an experience of God is achieved." [7] In this viewpoint as expressed, Elliott chose to continue to align himself with the liberalist positions that had been well established and dominant for many years — in fact, for so long that scarcely anyone had raised a voice of protest or challenge against them. The difference between Elliott and his immediate predecessors in religious education theorizing was that he dared to raise the question, based on a thorough study of the neoorthodox positions, especially Emil Brunner's, which he found it necessary to reject. There was rejoicing in the liberalist camp that Elliott had emerged to champion the long-accepted cause against the theological "reactionaries." Ernest J. Chave, of The University of Chicago, for example, was of the opinion that "a careful study of this book should lead to fruitful conferences in which antagonisms might be eliminated and combined ministries give new meaning to the Christian cause." [8] Chave was able to say applaudingly, "Elliott proves that religious education can be Christian," because Elliott had come out with a definition of what it is to be a Christian that was eminently acceptable to the defenders of the educational precincts against the neoorthodox theologians.

THE CHALLENGE: *H. Shelton Smith*

Once having been raised, that question was bound to lead into a debate which would last long and move into as yet unforeseen channels. One amazing fact is that *the* rejoinder came almost at once. Although H. Shelton Smith's *Faith and Nurture* was not conceived primarily as a reply to Elliott's thesis, it is obvious that Professor Smith, of Duke University, had been grappling with identical questions concurrently and had come out at the opposite pole. He had seen Elliott's book prior to the publication of his own work, for he cited it in numerous footnotes.

This was H. Shelton Smith's motive for writing:

That the modern movement in Protestant religious education is confronted with a crucial decision in its theological orientation can hardly be denied. The necessity for making a decisive choice derives from the emergence of post-liberal patterns of religious thought which now challenge the central assumptions and concepts of liberal Christian nurture. The question therefore has arisen: Shall Protestant nurture realign its theological foundations with the newer currents of Christian thought, or shall it resist those currents and merely reaffirm its faith in traditional liberalism? [9]

Professor Smith makes a careful analysis of the historical roots of the American Protestant liberalism that found expression in the religious education movement of the first decades of the twentieth century. His listing of the " historic tendencies of liberalism " succinctly summarizes the cardinal emphases that found classic expression in writers like George Albert Coe: divine immanence; the idea of growth — growth of religion in the individual and in the race, as well as growth as a mode of achieving individual and social change; the essential goodness of man; the his-

torical Jesus. Smith shows how the writers in religious
education who themselves often denied the significance of
theology as such held to a theology as definite in *its* presuppositions as any theology might be. What are " the
assumptions, concepts, and tendencies of liberal faith "? [10]
How do these get expressed in pedagogical theory? With
deliberate and knifelike logical analysis that yet was
thorough and just, he lets these presuppositions stand revealed, permitting the writers' ideas to be expressed in
their very own words. He depicts a theological basis for
liberal nurture that usually is more derived from secular
philosophical positions than from Biblical or historical
roots. Thus, for example, he demonstrates how experi-
mentalist, democratic educational theory is inimical to the
type of religious faith on which Christian education must
rest unless its distinctive Christian foundations are to be
denied altogether.

In the light of the return to a theocentric, transcenden-
talist, Trinitarian theology, then, such as that which by
1940 was beginning to gain ascendancy in the American
theological scene after many generations of liberalism,
what course would be open to progressive religious educators? Thus we come back to the question with which
Professor Smith began his inquiry, as cited above.

Elsewhere, Smith stated as follows the alternatives that
were open to religious education theorists and practitioners: They could (1) continue their opposition to the neoorthodox tendencies, thus choosing to make a negative
witness; (2) align with metaphysical naturalism and aban-
don the distinctive Christian tradition altogether; (3) engage in a reconstruction of theological foundations.[11] As
we shall see, all three of these alternatives, in one form or
another, were taken up by the emerging new voices. It

was obvious to all where Smith himself stood.

Regretfully, from the standpoint of the rich intellectual resources he would have brought to the task, Smith turned his attention from religious education theory to other interests, especially the history of American religious thought, after the publication of *Faith and Nurture*. As the *Festschrift* in his honor at the time of his retirement from the faculty of Duke University indicated, "what he was after was a new theological climate, better suited to the swirl and convulsions of the modern world — in which new insights might emerge and be developed in the light of the longer and deeper experiences of the Christian community in space and time."[12] Although he did no further formal publication in Christian education theory as such, certainly this one book played an enormously important role in the rethinking of the theological bases for church education during the succeeding twenty years. The tremendous productivity of writers in this field, who in a real sense were responding to the challenge he set forth in *Faith and Nurture*, is a tribute to the seminal character of his book. He himself viewed his work as polemical or analytical, warning in his preface that the task of reconstruction would have to be undertaken later. Actually, this is exactly what *did* happen. The reconstruction was undertaken, sometimes defensively and sometimes tentatively, but sometimes in quite unexpected ways as well. There was not going to be any new consensus so strong as had been the agreements within the liberalistic religious education movement, but there was to be richness and depth of a new variety.[13]

Actually some new elements had started to exist in the worldwide church situation that were bound to alter the very reconstructive task itself. The old battles of literalism versus "free interpretation," or authoritarianism versus creativity, were to be viewed somewhat differently. On the horizon in 1940 were the rising tides of the ecumenical movement, in which churches met with other churches at the points of most intense and critical disagreement in order to discover the unity that underlay their differences. This was no longer to be merely a cooperative work in good causes, but an examination of the essential nature of the church in the light of God's intention for it. The liturgical movement was going to cause all branches of the church to reexamine the foundations of their cultic life and the very meaning of divine worship, as well as the relation of the church to the structures of the world. New philosophical interests were to supplant the comfortable personalism and pragmatism that had been assumed as ultimate for many of the previous leaders in religious education: existentialism and language analysis, for example, which only now are being seriously weighed for their implications for the theory of nurture. Meanwhile, too, a new form of the social gospel was going to arise out of the ashes of post-World War II Europe — a radical Christian witness expressed through evangelical academies, worker-priests, and Bonhoeffer's "religionless Christianity." Biblical theology was going to become a pervasive influence throughout the church; and the rediscovery of the Bible was going to go beyond merely a continuous examination of the text into the examination of many questions concerning the relevance of Biblical faith to man's life in the world.

All this added up to the beginning of a new era in Christian education. Meanwhile, the denominations were facing the new day in terms of providing new curricula for their churches, rethinking the role and the training of lay teachers, and rediscovering the dependence of the educational task on the whole life of the worshiping, working, witnessing community.[14]

Back of every practical decision made in the life of a denomination or a local parish, there must be some theoretical basis. The task of the theorists in Christian education is to set forth the theological, Biblical, psychological, and other foundations on which curriculum, leadership training, and all other aspects of the church's educational program may rest.

This present study is based on the premise that in its task of seeking an adequate education, the church is highly dependent on the work of individual writers. To be sure, blueprints and designs are drawn up by commissions and committees, and the ultimate program is worked out by practitioners at several stages of responsibility. But back of almost everything that gets figured out in headquarters are some ideas that were first developed in the minds and experiences of those who produced thoughtful books.

None of the persons engaged in the prolific writing that has emerged since 1940, surely, would claim to have said the last word. Yet because they have been productive on a level to delight the professors and students of Christian education, it would seem that now is the time to make an effort to sort out their ideas and to see some of the ingredients available to the church in its continuing search for an education.

Harrison Elliott saw the clouds of change forming on the horizon. H. Shelton Smith initiated, if not an earthquake, at least a major shake-up. The church throughout Christendom has been benefiting ever since from the response its educational theorists have been making in the effort to move into new directions. In the succeeding chapters we shall look at the various types of Christian educational thinking in the period since that watershed which *Faith and Nurture* now can be seen to have been.

2

The Liberalist Continuum

THE word "liberal" was attached to a theological outlook that emerged first during the nineteenth century
in Europe but reached its farthest stretch to the left during the height of the religious education movement of the
1920's and 1930's. As David W. Jewell has pointed out,
"liberalism" has two points of reference. For one thing,
the term refers to "a particular spirit or attitude toward both old traditions and new understanding, . . .
to receptivity to that which is new, to freedom from prior
commitments (save those to the liberal spirit), and to
the willingness to break through present structures of
thought or practice in order to formulate new patterns." [1]
This usage of the term is one of special meaning to many
in our modern society who feel that the preservation of
such a spirit is the *sine qua non* of a society of free persons. As *the liberal spirit,* this usage of the term appeals
to people from many and no religious traditions. It is a
way of thinking, an attitude of mind, rather than any set
of doctrines.

However, as Professor Jewell goes on to point out, the
term is used also "in referring to a particular body of doctrine giving a distinctive exposition of the basic beliefs

of Christians." The characteristic tenets of liberalism as a theological " system " include a stress on the following: the infinite dignity and value of man, who possesses unlimited potential for growth; the continuity of the divine Being with his creation (divine immanence); Jesus Christ as the prototype of man at his best and highest; Christianity regarded principally as an ethical religion, seeking social justice through the reconstruction of the forms of social organization; the church as an institution of society devoted to character development and social action; revelation as the progressive building up of a body of knowledge by which society and men might be transformed; the Bible as the record of the progressive development of man's religious consciousness; salvation by gradual growth in knowledge and self-control.[2]

Others have listed the characteristic emphases of liberalism in terms similar to those given by Jewell. For example, II. Shelton Smith states these tenets as including some additional views: spiritual values inherent in the total round of human events; a philosophy of history based on evolutionary growth; persons as living entirely within the kingdom of grace; God as the indwelling germ principle of the community of selves; the cosmos in continuous becoming; an optimistic view of the moral progress of the race.[3] Smith demonstrates how the leading exponents of the religious education movement, typified by George Albert Coe, took these liberalist tenets and linked them with some pedagogical assumptions from John Dewey in the cross-fertilization that came to dominate the movement. When Dewey spoke of the continuous reconstruction of experience, the need for purposeful self-expression on the part of the child, the school as being democracy's primary agent in social progress, and the students' own activities as being the unifying center of the curriculum, he was using concepts that sprang from a similar philosophical milieu as did those characterizing religious liberalism. The wedding of the liberal theology and the liberal educational theory can be said to have produced that species of liberalist religious education which Professor Smith insisted needed to be reexamined by the church in order that its real presuppositions might be uncovered.

Among the theorists of the period since 1940, some have taken the position that liberalism should not be written off as dead. The very theses advanced by the liberal religious educators, they feel, though indeed subject to continuous reexamination, will be found on inspection to hold up very well. Not only are these liberalist notions to be accepted as perennially valid but they are to be explored even further in order that their liberating influence might be sent forth into ever-wider sectors of the race.

Not all whom we might group together in the liberalist continuum would desire to be considered as thinking alike. In fact, there is healthy debate among them, and they write out of the different ecclesiastical contexts that color the manner in which their theses are presented. Still, there is sufficient affinity with the kind of emphases outlined by Jewell, Smith, and others as characteristically " liberal " views to permit us to venture this broad general classification.

NATURALISTIC RELIGIOUS EDUCATION:
Sophia Lyon Fahs

On the extreme left among the liberalists, theologically speaking, is Sophia Lyon Fahs. For many years Mrs. Fahs directed the experimentally-oriented church school at the

Riverside Church, New York City, while teaching religious education at Union Theological Seminary in the days of Coe and Elliott. In later years she became identified with the American Unitarian Association (now the Unitarian Universalist Association) as editor of *The New Beacon Series in Religious Education,* a curriculum for Sunday church schools of the Unitarian Universalist denomination. Dorothy Tilden Spoerl, one of Mrs. Fahs's associates in developing the curriculum, has said this of it: "Having no creed to impart, the aim of the series is to help the children develop an adequate philosophy of life, for which it is believed that it is necessary to help them develop sound and adaptable personality structure, and to give them an adequate background of the Judeo-Christian tradition, and a wide view of all the manifestations of religion man has developed, together with a knowledge of where their own denomination fits into this cultural stream." [4]

In her book *The Old Story of Salvation,* Mrs. Fahs sets forth a description of the seven great ages of time, according to Augustine, in which are depicted the Biblical schemata of God's redemptive activity. In her discussion of this material Mrs. Fahs displays scholarly competence and objective fairness. In fact, this is one of the most lucid depictions of the story of salvation extant. However, she makes her analysis in order to repudiate the story. She feels that this is indeed the way thousands and even millions of orthodox Christians still understand Bible history.[5] She would prefer, however, not to regard the Bible "as a unified book with one consistent 'salvation story' in it portraying the history and destiny of all mankind. Nor is the Bible studied to learn about God and what he said and did. It is studied to find out how a certain great people thought and felt and believed about God." [6]

Mrs. Fahs's principal work is entitled *Today's Children and Yesterday's Heritage.*[7] Its subtitle indicates the orientation of the work in terms of theological focus: " A Philosophy of Creative Religious Development." The word " creative " had been a favorite one for Coe and others.[8] By it they meant a free, untrammeled, pedagogical method springing from a view of the universe that was unwilling to accept any fencing in by doctrine or " authoritarian " attitudes. Later theologians and teachers were to question the appropriateness of using " creative " in this context, its original connotation always having been in reference to creation *ex nihilo* by God alone.[9] However, Mrs. Fahs and her colleagues in the curriculum endeavors with which she has been associated have placed a primary emphasis on the possibility of arriving at both a theological orientation and a teaching methodology that look outward and forward.

The " traditional ways of religious guidance " are contrasted with what she calls " the natural ways." The " traditional " ways are transmissive, authoritarian, and indoctrinating. In contrast, " the natural approach to religious development " puts an emphasis on emergence, change, newness. Between these two, Mrs. Fahs states, there are profound philosophical differences.[10]

In a chapter on " It Matters How We Gain Our Beliefs," she isolates what she feels is " the really vital issue . . . between the major divergent groups in religious education. In one group, religion is considered as something *given* to an individual by an authority other than himself, by an authority coming from the past — from revelation, from an inspired book, from a divine person, or from a divinely ordained church. Thus religion becomes a body of ' affirmations ' presented as ' truths ' to be understood, appreciated, and accepted." [11]

In contrast, the other group holds to a conception of religious development admittedly less commonly held. " For them beliefs regarding the universe and man's destiny in it should be the products of maturing emotional experiences, meditation and critical thought, and not assumptions with which to begin. Religion is, therefore, not a heritage which the child has a God-given right to receive, not something to be imparted to him by a teacher or a group. Rather it is regarded as a vital and healthy result of his own creative thought and feeling and experience as he responds to life in all its fullness." [12]

Mrs. Fahs's overwhelming concern with a free, untrammeled approach to religious nurture leads her to be highly critical of all the inherited methods of teaching religion. She regards two of these as having been characteristic of time past and now unworthy for continuing use, since they are both " traditional " and " authoritarian." These two suspect methods are the use of Bible stories with young children and the induction of children into religious beliefs through ceremonials. She fears that the use of such methods will make religion appear to the growing mind of the child as essentially words to be said, postures to be observed, external rituals to be performed. The end result of this process would be to have people trained in using words and actions without meaning. Furthermore, instead of bringing members of our society together in universally held symbols, such vocabularies and actions would only perpetuate divisiveness within society.[13]

All of this objection to " indoctrination in beliefs " and " habit-training in ceremonials " rests ultimately upon a very high regard for the milieu of " a dynamic democratic society," in which she thinks religion should be a contributing factor. The identification of Christianity with democracy, as we have seen, was a pervasive interest of religious education leaders in the earlier part of this century, and in this emphasis Mrs. Fahs displays a liberalist continuum.

Along with this respect for the social milieu in which creative, nonauthoritarian goals should always be providing the social initiative goes a characteristic set of ideas concerning the uses of the past, the place of the individual, and the importance of reason.

What are the uses of the past? The past is to be explored only because it illumines the present. " It is for the sake of understanding present problems in order to solve them wisely that youth needs to be aware of the past." [14] An illustration of this would be the way in which a knowledge of the ancient struggle over the conquest of Canaan will throw light on the emotional struggles between Jews and Arabs since the formation of the modern state of Israel. This is an instrumentalist view of the past, one that Mrs. Fahs shares with the Dewey-Coe insistence on an education involving the continuous reconstruction of experience.

The importance of the individual is not slighted in the concern for social wholeness and universalism. As a matter of fact, the individual is always kept in the foreground through the accent on religion as primarily " something created by cach individual." If our principal concern is with the question, " How is it possible for a child to build his own religion? " [15] it becomes extremely important to keep him as an individual continually in focus. This is not to suggest that Mrs. Fahs could agree with any concept of individualism in society that would make for economic or political right-wing conservatism. Her concern for the individual, rather, is that each person might be able to arrive at personal integrity and self-understanding in order to be able to enter into "satisfying human relationships" and "to understand the larger, strategic, emotional conflicts of our time." [16]

Likewise, the author places a great emphasis on the importance of believing — the rational faculty in man. As a matter of fact, she declares that "one's religious belief or one's 'religion' is the 'gestalt' of all his smaller specific beliefs. One's faith is the philosophy of life that gathers up into one emotional whole — and sometimes, although rarely, into a reasoned whole — all the specific beliefs one holds about many kinds of things in many areas of life." [17] Note that although she recognizes that the "reasoned whole" is seldom achieved in actuality, nevertheless that would be the desirable goal. It must be said, though, that due to her awareness of the psychological (and even the psychiatric) dimensions of human personality, she does not commit the error of letting her rationalistic interests ever verge on propositionalism, as was sometimes the case with educators who put a high premium on the training of the mind, such as Herbart, or, in a sense, Dewey. She certainly would subscribe to a problem-solving theory of educational methodology, but the problems *do* involve mystery and feelings as well as "right" ideas.

The criticism has been made of Mrs. Fahs that her rationalism is not rigid enough to prevent the intrusion of a certain degree of "nature mysticism" into her thinking. However, it *is* rigid in the sense that she introduces new intellectual absolutes in the place of indoctrination, which she repudiates, as, for example, when she rejects the "old story of salvation" as intellectually untenable, while assuming that man in modern times can create a satisfactory explanation of his world that will transcend naïve myth. If the allegation concerning an addiction to nature mysticism is to be substantiated, there would be no better way to do it than to cite a little story that she tells. A girl grows from the question, "Mother, do you think if we could fly out and out, instead of in, past all the sky and where the stars are, that we would come to where there is just God and not any world?" into a vast awareness of "the great ineffable Mystery, which she came to call 'the real God.'" Is her conclusion very close to pantheism? She writes: "God cannot be seen or touched or located or proved as a single fact. In God are gathered up all facts, all knowledge, all experiences, all thoughts, all feelings. . . . Vital religion lives in the totality of experience." [18]

To sum up, in Sophia Lyon Fahs we have a clear and unmistakable decision: to continue on the liberal way — in fact, not only to stay by it, but to take it to its as yet undisclosed termination. [19]

PERSONALISTIC LIBERALISM: *Harry C. Munro*

If in Sophia Lyon Fahs the liberalist stream is manifested at the extreme left, in Harry C. Munro we observe it much more to the center, if not to the right of center. The late Dr. Munro was a minister of the Disciples of Christ and served for many years as a professor in church-related colleges, notably in Brite College of the Bible, Texas Christian University.

He chose to write *Protestant Nurture: An Introduction to Christian Education* against the background of certain questions that seemed to him of paramount importance: "What is the real nature of the crisis that confronts West-

ern Christian civilization? What responsibility have Protestant Christians in meeting that crisis? What kind of education will enable Protestant Christians to achieve the
real genius of their spiritual heritage, and thus qualify for
such a responsibility? " [20] Another set of his preliminary
questions brings his perspective directly into the midst of
the dialogue with which contemporary religious education has been involved since Smith's challenge: " How do
recent developments in American theological thinking
affect our conception of Christian nurture? How do developments in the psychology of personality and the theory
of character bear upon our interpretation of Christian
education? What reconstruction of Protestant churches
from within is required to qualify them for their present
educational and social responsibility? " [21] It is noteworthy
that Dr. Munro chose to frame all his chapter headings
as well as the subheadings within chapters in the form of
questions. Did he thereby intend to avoid the seemingly
indicative statement, seeking to serve some mediatorial
role? Or was this done out of a genuine conviction that it is
the educator's function primarily to raise queries?

Like his precursors in the liberalist school, Munro sets
his argument in terms of the democratic-authoritarian
tension. He sees Christianity on the side of the democratic
view and way, as over against the pretenses of authoritarianism in its various contemporary guises. He sees the
present situation as representing a " retreat into authoritarianism," characterized by a too great desire for security
and accompanied by an avoidance of individual responsibility, the denigration of the rights of the common man,
institutions conceived as a means for the control of the
masses, and the resting of knowledge on a set of a priori
assumptions closed to examination or open questioning.

In contrast, democracy tries to insist at all times on the freedom and self-realization of responsible persons, each person as the measure of all other values, institutions as designed for the service and enrichment of the persons involved, and truth as publicly available.[22]

Munro rests his case for the democratic way on the ground that " all men are equal before God. His laws are written in the moral order of the universe. . . . All men are equally responsible for living according to their best understanding of these laws." [23] Unlike Coe, who had preferred the term " democracy of God " to "kingdom of God," Munro does accept God as a sovereign ruler, who does not need to stand for reelection, and who would still be ruler of the universe even though his kingship were completely rejected by men.

Already we see one of Munro's characteristic emphases: the validity of the Christian explanations of life and the universe is deeply dependent upon the human situation. He looks at the Christian way with an eye to its relevance to human concerns at every level, and, in a measure, attests its truth in pragmatic terms. Protestant Christianity is " an emphasis upon the worth and dignity of the individual person as based upon his direct filial relationship with God. It was an Emancipation Proclamation for the mind and the spirit of man." [24] At the same time, it must be asserted that he is careful to point out how man's undoing is bound up with his self-concern and pride, and he recognizes, along with classical orthodox Christian theology, that " self-sufficient finitude " is the foundation of sin.

Dr. Munro shows his liberalist orientation in his choice of frequently used phrases, such as " prophetic religion," " universal God," and " principle." Asking, " What is the faith we teach? " he answers that to understand Christian faith, we must pay attention to at least four " sources of information and insight." These he lists as: " the specific actions of God in human history through which he has made himself known to men and has sought to bring them into responsible and filial relationships with himself; the coming of Jesus of Nazareth into the life of mankind as the Incarnation of God and the revealer of God's character and will; the continued life of the risen and living Christ as Savior and Redeemer of mankind; the meanings which the Christian faith has accumulated through the experiences of those who have sought to live by it during the centuries of Christian history." [25] He recognizes that all four of these are important, but as his principal focal point he selects Jesus Christ as revealer of God's character and will. Although he uses incarnational language, his subsequent elucidation of the role of Christ clearly shows where he puts his primary accent — on Jesus as being the fulfillment of the prophetic tradition: " He carried to its climax their interpretation of a universal ethical monotheism in terms of a Father-God of all mankind." [26] If we needed further support for this identification, we could cite numerous other examples of statements throughout the book indicating an understanding of the incarnation in moral or volitional terms. For example, he quotes approvingly Harry Emerson Fosdick's reference to Jesus' special contribution as being the " champion of personality," and George Albert Coe's famous definition of Christian education as " the systematic, critical examination and reconstruction of relations between persons, guided by Jesus' assumption that persons are of infinite worth, and by the hypothesis of the existence of God, the Great Valuer of Persons." [27]

When it comes to his discussion of the educational process, Munro clearly espouses a type of teaching that is akin to the " creative " principles enunciated by Mrs. Fahs. Like her, he rejects any " education of imposition, fixing its attention upon passing on a ready-made holy book, or body of revealed truth, or sacred institution, or set of behavior patterns," on the ground that such an education would tend to separate " teaching from the kind of vital, firsthand experience which would give its content valid meaning." [28]

Placing Dr. Munro's theological orientation is made more complicated by the fact that often he uses traditionalist terminology, though his meaning, if examined carefully, is obviously liberalist. He suggests that his approach might well be called " Christ-centered." In his analysis of what he means by this phrase, we discover that he intends to bring the person into relationship with the historical Jesus — his character and attitudes especially. The Old Testament is to be interpreted as the Bible that Jesus knew. His life shows us " the best and most successful way of living " in God's world. " Education can indeed be Christ-centered in just the degree that it succeeds in making Christ a vivid personal experience for each person." [29] Still, there is no doubt that compared with Sophia Lyon Fahs, Dr. Munro is a " conservative liberal " indeed. He is definitely within that American Protestant tradition which would identify itself as Trinitarian, Biblically-oriented, and Christ-focused, though these categories are almost invariably interpreted in terms of a personalistic liberalism that would prefer not to be couched in the historic creedal forms. He wants a " creative, life-centered type of Christian education " that will embody a " venturesome experimental spirit." [30]

A THIRD TYPE OF LIBERALISM?

We have seen above how two writers have taken their educational stance within the general category of liberalist Christian thought. One perspective is frankly naturalistic. The other prefers to use orthodox terminology but puts an accent similar to the naturalistic view on the theological assumptions from which to proceed.

Within recent years a third type of liberalist thought has been identified by some as "neoliberalism." This is not an organized movement, but several characteristic emphases have appeared in some theological writing that mark this off from either of the types of liberalist thought we have considered.

A leading exponent of this neoliberal school is L. Harold DeWolf, professor of systematic theology in Boston University School of Theology for many years and now dean of Wesley Theological Seminary, Washington, D.C. He himself has identified these emphases: a recognition that neoorthodox teachings were a needed corrective to extreme liberal rationalism, but an insistence that reason should not be underestimated as the receiver and interpreter of revelation; revelation regarded not as absolutely confined to the Biblical tradition; immanence of God coexistent with his transcendent Being; the Kingdom of God understood as dependent on God's initiative but as involving the faithful obedience of men in all aspects of their existence; a recognition that though man was in bondage to sin, his acceptance by God makes him the vehicle of God's grace.[31]

These distinctive accents of neoliberalism have not yet been translated systematically into Christian educational theory, though Professor DeWolf himself has shared some of his theological insights in relation to Christian teaching in *Teaching Our Faith in God*.[32] Unlike Mrs. Fahs, who rejected the " old story of salvation," considering it irrelevant for man today and tomorrow, DeWolf is willing to see the Fall as reenacted in every person: " Such re-enactment of the Fall seems to occur in every life on the road from innocence to maturity. It looks as if maturity could not be reached without falling into sin." But he says, " We must check ourselves here." This checking marks him as belonging to the liberalist school. " Only when the individual's expression of his freedom overreaches its proper bounds, does he sin." [33] Perhaps it is too wide a category to embrace both Fahs and DeWolf, with Munro in between — but it does appear that to do so is not to overstretch the several definitions of liberalism with which we began this chapter.

3

Psychologically-oriented Nurture

I T IS no coincidence that religious educators should have
been concerned for many years with the psychological
dimensions of human experience. However one may think
theologically regarding the place of man in the created
order and in the scheme of salvation, the fact is that real
persons are necessarily involved in the drama of salvation.
If God is to be recognized, reverenced, and responded to,
it will be by and in persons that such processes occur.
Thus the nature of the human being, his inner psychic
phenomena, the workings of his mind, are germane to the
educative task within the religious community.

Indeed, Johann Friedrich Herbart (1776–1841), Kant's
successor in the chair of philosophy at the University of
Königsberg and the founder of " scientific " modern modes
of teacher training, pioneered in psychology. He was
deeply concerned with religious nurture and was a committed Christian. As he developed his interests in education, he realized that very little was known, actually, about
the persons whom education was seeking to educate. He
did some early researches into the relation of the consciousness to the unconsciousness (long before Freud) and
the question as to how ideas arise in the human mind. He

is famous for having set forth a theory of the way in which new ideas emerge from material already mastered — apperception, as he called it — and he undertook investigations into the way in which learning takes place, thus becoming one of the earliest of the modern theorists of learning. His " five steps " — preparation, presentation, comparison, generalization, and application — were not originally a neat technique for lesson planning, as later they were often interpreted, so much as they were a scheme whereby the manner of the pupil's learning could be met by pedagogical arrangements. That, he thought, was the way to proceed in teaching because these steps corresponded to the ways in which pupils learned.[1] These facts about Herbart are mentioned simply to show how education and psychology were bound up from the very beginning of the modern science of psychology. And even long before that, teachers and writers on education from the Greeks onward had been deeply concerned with psychological questions.

The realm of psychology is the realm of human experience. The investigation of the human psyche can proceed quite apart from any dependence on theological presuppositions, though theological questions are implicit in any investigation of the human psyche. Whereas theologians grappled for centuries with all kinds of problems related to the " soul " of man, psychologists, once psychology became a separate and autonomous science, were unwilling to assume even such a reality as " soul." But all of them, in various ways, were deeply immersed in the experiential as over against the purely theoretical or abstract.

When Sigmund Freud set forth a delineation of the unconscious in terms of a theory of psychoanalysis, he was motivated to a large degree by clinical interests and concerns. The branch of medicine that came to be known as psychiatry was motivated primarily not by any desire to create a system of thought but by the effort to cure mentally disturbed patients. Before the rise of modern psychiatry much of the treatment of such persons had been based on guesswork, backed up by little cumulative, clinically-tested knowledge. From now on, the climate was going to deal increasingly in " depth." Religious educators were slow to look to this " depth " dimension in psychology, since they had established their affinities more definitely with the laboratory research type of psychology which had put an emphasis on behavior that could be outwardly discerned. The so-called " behavioristic " psychology of the 1920's and 1930's seemed to meet an echoing response in some aspects of the liberalist theology. On the other hand, the " depth " psychologies of the later years now became attractive to theologians. This was due to the fact that the kind of complex human being that depth psychology was revealing was more in keeping with the sinful, alienated man who was emerging into theological consideration through the influence of Biblical theology.

Earl A. Loomis has described this type of psychology thus:

Whatever the meaning of " depth " in our concepts of depth psychology, it is clear that when man is viewed in depth, he is viewed multidimensionally. This means that no single cross-section of his behavior is self-explanatory but that everything is influenced by and influences everything else. It means that man is a complex being and that what passes for evil as well as good is part of his reality that cannot be ignored but must somehow be incorporated into his complete self-discovery and self-fulfillment. It means, moreover, that if human beings are to find resonance with other creatures of depth — amphibiously, to use Aldous Huxley's term — human groups and society must have access to depth perception, depth communication, and depth resistance. By the latter is meant that those who face the depths in themselves and others face a dramatic threat, one, indeed, that is even more than dramatic: it is also potentially lethal. To survive this invasion from below and within, demands neither isolation nor merger but a dynamic interrelatedness within which growth can happen. It is to this adventure that depth psychology dedicates itself. It is from this adventure that depth psychology draws its strength.[2]

Meanwhile, in the life of the churches and in the theological seminary curriculum this new dimension of psychology was bearing fruit in a revitalized theology and practice of pastoral care. It was being discovered that many of the traditional approaches to pastoral life — miscellaneous parish calling, routine visits to the sick, conferences regarding imminent baptisms, marriages, or funerals — were no longer adequate to cope with the actual frustrations, problems, needs, and cravings — conscious and unconscious — obviously determining the real lives of people. Pastoral theology was to utilize many insights derived from psychology and psychiatry in the period immediately following World War II. Practically every theological seminary would require its bachelor of divinity candidates to undergo a period of clinical training in general or mental hospitals, where they would be confronted with human needs in extremest forms. Against this human situation they could then learn to see themselves more clearly as equally complex beings, though called to be ministers of God's grace to others in need. Through such training, followed by carefully planned seminars back in the schools, prospective ministers and other religious workers would learn to rise above utilitarian, moralistic " solutions," always too easy and invariably inadequate, as well as to have a more modest expectation of their own effectiveness in counseling roles. At the same time, they would be released into greater effectiveness by virtue of this exposure to their own limitations and shortcomings. A whole new literature (variously referred to as " pastoral counseling " or " pastoral theology ") was to be produced during the next decades by scholars of the caliber of Carroll Wise, Seward Hiltner, William Hulme, Wayne Oates, and Granger Westberg.

Some of these psychologically-oriented pastoral theologians began to extend their concerns into the field of Christian education, which, too, was now open to the reconstructive task that religious educators saw was necessary to essay. In some cases the cross-fertilization of interests and ideas was furthered by the fact that the churches were beginning to produce new curricula for their Sunday church schools. Knowing of the need for " depth " understandings informed by contemporary psychological understandings, curriculum editors tended to look to the new group of pastoral theologians for counsel and specific suggestions.[3]

EDUCATION THROUGH ACCEPTANCE:

Reuel L. Howe

One of these curricular efforts was initiated by the Department of Christian Education of the Protestant Episcopal Church, an effort that eventuated in a total curriculum called *The Church's Teaching* (formerly known as *The Seabury Series*). The leaders of the Department realized that a necessary preliminary to their church's ac-

ceptance of a dynamic new curriculum would be the preparation of the people to see that Christian education is
more a matter of the total life of the church than just
the use of curriculum materials as such. Thus a team of
theologians and educators was organized to make extensive appearances throughout the country. One of those
invited to participate was Reuel L. Howe, who at that
time (the early 1950's) was professor of pastoral theology
in the Protestant Episcopal Theological Seminary in
Alexandria, Virginia. For many years he had been involved
in the Council for Clinical Training as well as in parish
life. It was out of these team presentations that Dr. Howe
evolved the material that eventuated in *Man's Need and
God's Action*.[4] Upon publication, that book was widely
disseminated in the Protestant Episcopal Church as an
adult study guide, and it eventually had great influence in
curricular orientation among several other denominations
as well, notably the United Church of Christ.

Since Reuel Howe talks a great deal about relationship
between God and man, and between man and man, it
might seem confusing to see him described here as " psychologically-oriented " instead of being included in the
next chapter, where we shall speak of " education through
relationship." The reason for including him in the present
category — admittedly an arbitrary decision — is that
throughout his work he has displayed a primary concern
with the implications of psychology for theology. When
he speaks of " relationship," indeed, it is in psychological
terms. This is evident in his description of the task he set
himself in his book:

Here is the question for which we all want an answer. " How
may the love of God be an answer for me? " I am going to try
to interpret God's answer to this question in the language of

today's experience. . . . Before the answer can become clear
we will have to ask and answer other questions.

First, "What do you want? What do you *really* want? What
moves you from day to day, week to week, month to month,
year to year? What is it for which you would sell everything
else? "

When we begin searching, we find that there are many answers. Some of our wants are immediate and superficial, some
of them are deeper; but the deepest one of all is the desire *to
be at one with someone, to have someone who can be at one
with us, and through whom we can find at-oneness with all.*[5]

Howe dwells at length on the experience of estrangement, a concept that the theologian Paul Tillich did much
to bring into current parlance. Alienation, separation —
these are what " estrangement " means. In relation to our
incapacity to love fully, or to be loved fully, we stretch
out, desperately looking for help. It is exactly " in relation
to this need for at-oneness " that the gospel is good news.
" God gave Himself in Jesus of Nazareth as the Personal
Answer to man's need. Our task now is to understand and
respond to God's action in terms of our need. . . . Our understanding of God's action will reveal to us who we are
and what we ought to be doing. Out of our needs we will
ask deep questions. As we ask these questions, we will
begin to hear His Answer. And as we begin to understand
His Answer, we will be able to ask better questions that
will lead to more comprehension of the ultimate answer." [6]

Here, it will be observed, Howe is using Tillich's " principle of correlation ": " A way of uniting message and
situation. It tries to correlate the questions implied in the
situation with the answers implied in the message." [7]
The human situation represents our actual psychological
state at any given time. It is to this that the gospel of

Jesus Christ speaks, he affirms. It is only the awareness of our being accepted even though we are unacceptable — and that without any merit on our part or through any work we can present — that will enable us to live in relation to others as true persons.

Like others who have highlighted the tendency to dehumanize mankind in modern civilization by virtue of our preoccupation with techniques and processes, Howe warns that when we use persons and treat them as things, we hurt both them and ourselves, perpetuating estrangement. Through Jesus Christ the psychological order is reversed: we are able to love persons *as* persons and use things *as* things.

Growing out of his pastoral theological orientation is Reuel Howe's penetrating analysis of the "most fundamental and crucial experiences of human life: . . . the common ventures of life to which all men are called and to which, if they live, they must make some kind of response." [8] In each of these he sees the "principle of correlation" at work, for the Christian faith offers an answer to the kind of question each of these crucial experiences induces. The implicit question of birth, for example, is, "How shall I find the full meaning of life?" To this, Christianity offers the initiatory rite of Baptism, "by means of which we are reborn into the relationship that has the promise implicit in the phrase 'Child of God.'" The experience of growth is met by the church's ministry of instruction, "part of the Christian Church's response to the obligations assumed at the time of baptism." Adolescence (transition from childhood to adulthood) is met by confirmation; the impulse toward mating by matrimony; parenthood ("who is equal to this responsibility?") by "some rite or ministry" offering "the redeeming and completing

power of the Divine Father "; sickness by the healing of
prayer; bereavement and death by the burial rites and
teaching that affirms " faith in being in the face of human
non-being." [9] He sees the Sacrament of Baptism as pivotal
in the process. Baptism initiates us into " a relationship
of the redeemed and the redeeming; of the forgiven and
the forgiving; of those who freely give out of what they
have freely received; of those who, having surrendered
themselves, have become the instruments of His saving
love; of those who, though broken and sinful, by Him
are used to heal and save." The church is thus seen to
be " the reconciling fellowship." [10]

Howe believes that " the problem of acceptance " is true
for everyone. At this juncture in his interpretation we see
how he uses psychological insight to illuminate the theological dimension. He draws on the child psychologists for
the insight that a child needs parental acceptance (" and
acceptance is an expression of love ").[11] He understands
that self-rejecting persons have difficulty in accepting
others. He knows that security is a " by-product of being
accepted." He goes on to suggest that the Christian understanding of acceptance is religious rather than " wholly
psychological "; that is, " it has to do with the very nature
of our being." Yet the religious seems also to continue to
be understood in terms of the psychological, for he interprets the forgiveness one receives from God in these
terms: " Only when we are secure and have the assurance
of acceptance dare we be honest about what we are and
are not. A relationship of security does not solve our
problems but it frees us from anxiety about ourselves and
helps us see and use our resources that are necessary if
we are to deal constructively with our problems." And
he suggests that Calvin understood justification by faith

to mean acceptance that comes from God.[12] In other words, the theological understanding tends here to be couched in psychological terms, and vice versa.

It is possible that Reuel Howe's appeal has been strong, at least in part, because he speaks in terms that former devotees of the older liberalism can still understand. The transition from secularistically-oriented terminology to the classical theological nomenclature as revived by neo-orthodoxy is sometimes very difficult for those who wish to move from the earlier, liberalist positions but who fear to leap too far. The facts seem to be that Howe has a firm orthodox basis for his thought and that his terminology can be used more easily by many groups because of its psychologically-oriented slant, with many overtones and undertones. At any rate, Howe was criticized by some of his fellow Episcopal churchmen on the ground that he did not pay enough attention to the sinful nature of the needs and wants of man; that he did not adequately interpret the ontological change that takes place in Baptism (not a mere altering of relationship, but one who was not previously a child of God is now made such); and that the stringent notes of the gospel are reduced into the one note of loving-kindness (overlooking, e.g., such " hard sayings " as Matt. 10:21). That criticism, however, came not from a source so much neoorthodox as from the Anglo-Catholic stance within the Protestant Episcopal Church.[13]

Reuel Howe continued his interests in pastoral theology after leaving his teaching position in Virginia. For some years he has headed the Institute for Advanced Pastoral Studies at Bloomfield Hills, Michigan, an interdenominational agency for stimulating dialogue in the areas where pastoral theology and religious education overlap. He has continued to follow an educational line of approach within his pastoral studies, as evidenced by his later books, *Herein Is Love, The Creative Years,* and *The Miracle of Dialogue.*[14] Like *Man's Need and God's Action,* these later books are informed with the same psychological orientation that has characterized his educational interests across the years.

This pastoral theological-psychological " overlap " is indicated in some words of an essay by Dr. Howe published in 1960: " The work of pastoral theology is barely begun. The dialogue between theology and the social sciences, between the human question and Gospel answer, between theory and practice, between the church and the world, between God and man, must and will continue. And only out of that dialogue will come the answer to the problems and questions of our own age." What are some of these questions to which the whole answer is as yet not apparent? In the same essay he lists some of them. " What is the meaning of the Christian faith in our time? What is the Christian style of life for the twentieth century? Where will we find the symbols that will bring together the meanings of God and the meanings of men? What image should we have of the church, of the ministry, of ourselves as ministers, that will liberate the dialogue between the church and the world? What image of the church will free the church of its preoccupation with its own welfare so that it can sense its God-given purpose in the world? By what process of education can we make available the insights of social dynamics and structures so that they will be relevant in our ministry to the social order — as psychological insights have aided the individual in primary relationships? " [15]

Is it possible, in the light of questions like these, that Reuel Howe, using the " system " of thought that now has become closely related to his viewpoint, will be moving from the psychological-personal level farther into the realm of the psychological-social? Man *solo* and man *corporate* both have educational tasks that can be further illuminated from psychology.

SELFHOOD, ENCOUNTER, BECOMING:
Lewis Joseph Sherrill

The " depth " of psychology that informs Reuel Howe's position is drawn upon also by another significant theorist in Christian education, Lewis Joseph Sherrill. Dr. Sherrill, a native of Texas, began his teaching career in the field of religious education at his own theological alma mater, the Louisville Presbyterian Theological Seminary, in 1925, after a four-year pastorate in Covington, Tennessee. In 1930 he was elected dean of the Louisville seminary, and in 1950 he was called to be Skinner and McAlpin Professor of Applied Theology in Union Theological Seminary, New York.

After his death in 1957, *Religious Education* carried an article, " The Contribution of Lewis J. Sherrill to Christian Education," by Roy W. Fairchild, to which we shall have occasion to refer several times in this chapter. We are especially indebted to Professor Fairchild for his penetrating analysis of Sherrill's psychological orientation. Fairchild points out that Sherrill rejected the work of the experimental psychologists as the basis for his own effort in correlating psychology and Christian nurture; nor was he especially interested in the group of developmental psychologists whose interest was the painstaking description of " the minutiae of behavior at different stages of life. Instead, while he did not quite ignore other schools, Sher-

rill turned to *psychoanalysis* as the major source of insight
into the nature of man. And when you cast about for a
reason for Sherrill's selectivity at this point, one suggests
itself immediately: *Psychoanalysis describes the kind of
human nature to which the Gospel speaks. . . .* In contrast to the experimentalists, psychoanalysts speak not of
isolated reflexes but of total responses; not of detachment
but of participation as a means of gaining knowledge; not
of mathematical formulae for human behavior but the
language of relationships." [16]

Fairchild shows how five basic psychological understandings of the " depth " variety were appropriated into
Sherrill's educational thinking: (1) auxiety; (2) perception; (3) relationship; (4) ambivalence; (5) identification. The educational process is not a simple matter. It
must deal with the existential realities of the human situation, to use Tillich's insistent argument. Sherrill was
always alert to the implications of dynamic psychology
for Christian teaching and learning, because he was un-
satisfied with the too-easy solutions that sometimes seemed
to preoccupy the attention of those whose " science " was
insufficiently penetrating to allow for ambiguity and po-
larity.

In 1953, Sherrill published the first of two books that
especially, among his writings, display his particular psychological orientation. This was *The Struggle of the Soul.*
In that book Sherrill suggests that there are three attitudes
toward life with corresponding "types": (1) life as a
treadmill, in which meaningless repetitiveness is the only
outcome, with ennui and hopelessness; (2) life as a *saga*,
in which man goes out as man to do battle against the
odds that seem to threaten him, issuing in the celebration
of the heroic potentialities in man on the purely human-

istic level; (3) life as a *pilgrimage*, in which the events of human existence are seen as lived out in relation to God, who gives meaning, purpose, and destiny to all experiences of the daily round. The Christian understanding, of course, will build upon the image of life as pilgrimage. In this pilgrimage, life consists of a succession of events that he regards as crises: times in which one can either go ahead with confidence or shrink back in fear. The deepest learnings take place in these times of crisis and our reaction to them.

The second book, *The Gift of Power*, was published in 1955. A bulletin of the Pastoral Psychology Book Club, cited by Professor Fairchild, gives us the background out of which the book was written, in Sherrill's own words:

In the truest sense, the basis of this book was rooted in my earliest days in the pastorate, thirty-five years ago. It was in those early days following graduation from the seminary that I realized an area of serious deficiency in my ministry. My theological background seemed miles apart from life situations in the parish. Furthermore, those were days when many of us seemed primarily concerned about an apology for and defense of the Bible.

I sensed my inability to come to grips with the actual problems that people faced. Some of the young people of the community were irresponsible and unmanageable, and there was the stark reality of more than a few suicides. Neither my theology nor psychology was fully adequate to cope with these circumstances. It was convincingly clear that I lacked the necessary insights into human action to deal with such tragic circumstances in a vitally helpful way.

Gradually I sensed the redemptive value of a strong bond of relationship. This ministry, if it was to be effective, must be more than a matter of perfunctory teaching and preaching. In the early twenties I resolved to bring content into that "more than " decision. It occurred to me that a deeper search must be made into the meaning of the Bible, of theology, of man, and of the most effective ways of communicating through preaching and teaching. This quest has led to exciting new discoveries, and continues to open new vistas constantly.

. . . For the past ten years I have especially sought to discern the basis for a philosophy of Christian community which was consistent with the depth dimension of revelation on the one hand, and the human predicament on the other. Upon reaching a workable basis in each area, it became necessary to develop a depth dimension of communication whereby the gap between the two could be bridged.[17]

It can be seen, especially from the last sentence in the quotation, how Sherrill was seeking to understand " depth " theology — " the depth dimension of revelation " — in relation to " depth " psychology — " the human predicament." The two, he realized, needed to be linked in terms of a " depth " dimension of communication consonant with the depth of either pole. It is as if he is speaking of deep calling unto deep — and visualizing the process of the movement itself from deep to deep as participating in the depth. This is another form of the " dialogue " or " principle of correlation " of which Howe speaks, as we have seen.

The process itself takes place in the twofold relation between man and God which he calls " confrontation " and " encounter." It is " confrontation " from God's side. That is, God takes the initiative. " To speak thus of ' confrontation ' means that God as infinite Personal Being faces man as a finite personal being. . . . To speak of revelation as God's *Self*-disclosure implies that *what* is revealed in the encounter between man and God is not information *about* God, but God *himself* as Personal Being. The reports of revelation may have to be cast in terms that contain information, or that attempt to describe what was perceived in the encounter. . . . Revelation is revelation to *human beings*." [18]

From man's side we would speak of "encounter." This is man's experience of being confronted by God. To put it another way, again in his own words: "A relationship between man and God is thus disclosed wherein man can retreat still further from God, or can move in the core of his being toward God. . . . Within such an encounter the rift within man himself can be healed, so that in being reconciled with God he is reconciled with himself." [19]

Sherrill then offers a definition of Christian education as "the attempt, ordinarily by members of the Christian community, to participate in and to guide the changes which take place in persons in their relationships with God, with the church, with other persons, with the physical world, and with oneself." [20] This process is undertaken with the aid of the Bible, which he construes as describing "a continuing confrontation, continuing throughout human history, throughout the life of every religious community, and throughout the life of every individual person from birth to death." The Bible is thus no mere record of past history. It is the means that symbolizes for the Christian the continual confrontation-encounter in which he finds the meaning of existence. In the Bible he finds "themes" — aspects of God's self-disclosure — that speak to man's predicaments at various stages of his life span. Each of these Biblical themes he sees as corresponding to "some profound human predicament": lordship, vocation, judgment, redemption, re-creation, providence, the life of faith.[21]

In Lewis J. Sherrill, Christian educators were faced

with a thoroughgoing analysis of the challenge of "depth" psychology to the understanding of the educative process, the nature of the curriculum, and the role of faith. No one heretofore had made so complete an exploration of the implications of such an interaction. In one sense the entire Christian educational literature of this period of history has been an effort to deal with Sherrill's central thesis, namely, that "the Christian religion can teach men how to receive a gift of interior, spiritual power sufficient to enable them to cope with the gift of exterior, physical power which has been granted. . . . In its simplest terms this means that the power which can be received is the power to become a self who can cope with itself in the modern world, and with the world in which we must live."[22] What is the nature of the "gift"? How shall the gospel be communicated? It is in writers like Sherrill that Christian education moves into the larger field of the whole communicative task. The boundaries between disciplines seem to vanish.

Some who feel that the psychological orientation has been overstressed in Howe and Sherrill would raise questions like these: Can the rather modest (and even, in some cases, questionable) institutions of religious education that the church has seen fit to employ across the years be regarded as capable of sustaining so lofty an educational effort? For example, to what extent can volunteer, lay teachers, themselves victims of existential anxiety in our present-day culture, be expected to develop enough sensitivity to be able to deal safely with the emergent selfhood of their pupils?[23] Do psychiatrically-oriented educational goals overlook the rather more routine needs of persons whose involvement in existential anxiety may be far less a predicament than has been alleged? Does the use of the

Bible as the source of the " themes " related to man's predicament tend to impose a principle of selection that will
overlook some Biblical accents that do not neatly fit these
themes? In other words, does this tend to fragment the
Bible?

Those desiring to survey the full scope of Sherrill's work
will be interested also in his other books, especially *The
Opening Doors of Childhood, The Rise of Christian Education,* and *Guilt and Redemption.* The first of these was
published prior to his later " depth " concerns. *The Rise
of Christian Education* is a solid piece of work which remains one of the best sources of information on Christian
education history through the medieval period. *Guilt and
Redemption* deals profoundly with themes that are of
deepest concern to both psychology and theology.[24]

4

Education Through Relationship

I N THE LAST chapter it was noted that "relationship" is
a word much used by Christian education theorists with
a psychological orientation. In this chapter we shall discuss a group of leading theorists who, although they too
are sensitive to psychological dimensions, use "relationship" in so pervasive a sense that we can in effect isolate
them as a whole category of writers who espouse education *through* relationship.

The term "relationship theology" has come into use in
recent decades to describe the stance from which such a
type of educational theory moves. The genesis of the concept is rather complex, for it is compounded of many
things: Martin Buber's *I and Thou,* which has influenced
much theological thought of our time, both Jewish and
Christian; the renaissance in Biblical theology, which has
recovered the centrality of the covenant relationship, God
to man, man to God, manifested through Israel and Christ,
and the consequent changed relationships of man to man
within the covenant community; the liturgical movement,
which has recalled the Christian churches of all forms into
a renewed interest in the common rites which remind the
people constantly of the relation of their present action to

the historic actions of God in the past.

In defining "relationship theology," Randolph Crump Miller says that it "is a term used to describe both the sources of theological truth and the means of communicating it." [1] If we look at it that way, we can say that there is an interpretation of theology that is best expressed in terms of relationship; there is also a mode of communication — teaching — that grows out of such relationship and expresses itself concomitantly. A teacher who derives his strength for living and meaning for life from his relation to God will manifest a concern for relationship with his pupils.

DIALOGUE: Martin Buber

The seminal contribution made by the Jewish philosopher-theologian Martin Buber in his *I and Thou* [2] has to do with the essentiality of relationship. There is no true human existence in anyone when one is not in relation to something other than himself. Buber illustrates this by an incident from his boyhood (when he was eleven) in which he and a horse were involved. He used to spend the summer on his grandparents' estate. As often as he could do it without being noticed, he would "steal into the stable and gently stroke the neck of [his] darling, a broad dapple-grey horse." He says:

If I am to explain it now, beginning from the still very fresh memory of my hand, I must say that what I experienced in touch with the animal was the Other, the immense otherness of the Other, which, however, did not remain strange like the otherness of the ox and the ram, but rather let me draw near and touch it. When I stroked the mighty mane, sometimes marvellously smooth-combed, at other times just as astonishingly wild, and felt the life beneath my hand, it was as though the element of vitality itself bordered on my skin, something that was not I, was certainly not akin to me, palpably the other, not just another, really the Other itself; and yet it let me approach, confided itself to me, placed itself elementally in the relation of *Thou* and *Thou* with me. The horse, even when I had not begun by pouring oats for him into the manger, very gently raised his massive head, ears flicking, then snorted quietly, as a conspirator gives a signal meant to be recognizable only by his fellow-conspirator; and I was approved.[3]

He continues by describing the decay of this relationship with the horse once he became self-conscious about his hand's stroking the beast. " The game went on as before, but something had changed, it was no longer the same thing."

The relationship of dialogue is what some writers refer to as " the language of relationship." The dialogue does not necessarily have to be couched in words. Verbal exchange can be mere monologue, if only one speaks and the other does not really hear, or even if both speak and only one hears. Buber argues for sensitive reciprocity, a willingness to speak to the other and to hear what the other says to one. This should be true not only of interpersonal relations but also within the larger society. Collectivity is often mistaken for community. Collectivity is only a " bundling together " rather than " a binding " together. "Community, growing community, . . . is the being no longer side by side but *with* one another of a multitude of persons. And this multitude, though it also moves towards one goal, yet experiences everywhere a turning to, a dynamic facing of, the other, a flowing from *I* to *Thou*." [4]

In 1947 two essays [5] of Buber's dealing specifically with

educational questions were published in England. In the essay entitled " Education " we have an address given by Buber in 1925 at the Third International Educational Conference in Heidelberg, the theme of which was " the development of the creative powers in the child." Recalling in what sense the word " creative " was being used by educators during the 1920's, we are reminded by Buber's fresh twist of the term of the way in which Karl Barth began his Gifford Lectures. These Lectures are required, under the trust by which they are supported, to deal with " natural theology." Barth began by saying he did not believe in " natural theology " as usually understood, then proceeded to present his magnificent addresses. Here Buber does a similar thing. Quoting the theme of the conference, he says, " As I come before you to introduce it I must not conceal from you for a single moment the fact that of the nine words in which it is expressed only the last three raise no question for me." He proceeds to give his own profound interpretation of the term " creative." [6]

Buber posits " the existence of an autonomous instinct, which cannot be derived from others, whose appropriate name seems to me to be the ' originator instinct.' Man, the child of man, wants to make things. He does not merely find pleasure in seeing a form arise from material that presented itself as formless. What the child desires is its own share in this becoming of things: it wants to be the subject of this event of production." [7] By this he means something deeper than the urge toward busyness or activity. But even this " instinct of origination " is subjected to further scrutiny by Buber. He rejects as the purpose of education merely stimulating this " instinct," for always such would only prepare man for solitariness. There is another " instinct " — that for communion, and it is this which suggests the deeper levels of education.

Among the various types of education, Buber differentiates those which start from " compulsory rules " and those which allow pupils freedom. Neither is adequate by itself. What the educator does is to select from the multitudinous possibilities existing in the world those ingredients which can be used by the student, made an inner part of himself and his understanding. " At the opposite pole from compulsion there stands not freedom but communion. . . . Freedom in education is the possibility of communion." [8] What is required on the teacher's part is " experiencing the other side," [9] that is, being able to confer with the pupil as if from within his own experience and need. He calls this the " true inclusion of one another by human souls." [10]

In his second essay, " The Education of Character," given originally to the National Conference of Jewish Teachers of Palestine at Tel Aviv in 1939, he continues this line of thought. Education is not to be based on moral maxims or merely interpenetrating habits; it is a great character that should be kept in mind, one who acts " from the whole of his substance. That is, it is peculiar to him to react in accordance with the uniqueness of every situation which challenges him as an active person." [11] " Genuine education of character is genuine education for community." [12]

Buber's ideas, relatively simple in essence but paradoxically stated, are deeply penetrating. He takes education out of the realm of little exercises and neat systems and insists that it be viewed in terms of individual and communal responsibility for life and the world. He is not interested in specifics; as a philosopher he seeks basic principles, leaving the working out of these matters to the actual teachers (though it must not be forgotten that he

himself has spent much of his life as a university teacher).
One is reminded at this point of another parallel with Karl
Barth. I once attended a conference at Wuppertal at
which Barth was the star guest. Instead of lecturing, he
answered questions from the audience. Seated on the
platform near him were some of Germany's leading theologians. Somebody asked, " How do you teach to young
children these theological matters of which you speak? "
He smiled and replied, " That I must leave to Dr. Hammelsbeck," who sat by him and to whom he pointed in
friendly gesture. (Dr. Oskar Hammelsbeck is one of the
leading educators of the Lutheran Church in Germany,
heading one of the teachers training colleges).

The fact is that Buber has deeply affected the understandings of many prominent and influential theologians:
Jewish, Roman Catholic, and Protestant. Through them
his stress on relationship and community, and his other
distinctive concepts, have entered the thinking of religious education theorists of a wide variety of theological
positions. It has been an especially strong influence on
those to whom we shall now refer.

IN QUEST OF THE CLUE: Randolph Crump Miller

One of the first writers to respond to Shelton Smith's
challenge in *Faith and Nurture* in terms of a reconstructive effort was Randolph Crump Miller. He speaks of
Smith's book as having been " the chief stimulus to my
thought." In his Preface to *The Clue to Christian Education,* Professor Miller outlines the problem with which he
sought to wrestle. He wanted to find a theology for Christian education that could undergird the objectives, theory,
and methods. He also was captivated by the problem of

how best to relate content and method in an organic whole. Subsidiary problems that concerned him had to do with the need to integrate evangelism into the educational program and the need to get more parent participation in religious nurture. " I found as I thought upon the problem that the ' clue ' would be found in the relevance of theology to the whole of life, and that with this clue I could open the doors of the associated questions of method, evangelism, and parent cooperation." [13]

At the time he wrote *The Clue to Christian Education,* Randolph Miller was teaching religious education and pastoral theology at the Church Divinity School of the Pacific, a denominational seminary of the Protestant Episcopal Church, of which Miller is a presbyter. Shortly after his work appeared, he was elected to the faculty of the Divinity School of Yale University, where, earlier, he had taken his doctor of philosophy degree. His now new colleague, Paul H. Vieth, had long been active in the rethinking of religious education, and Miller expresses appreciation to Vieth for having been helpful.[14]

In addition to the " trilogy " referred to below, Miller has produced other books. *Education for Christian Living* immediately became a standard textbook for college and seminary courses in Christian education and was issued in a revised, second edition in 1963. *Your Child's Religion* is a more popular type of book, designed for parents.[15] He has also written books of a devotional character and for many years has been editor of *Religious Education,* the bimonthly journal of the Religious Education Association, which, under his leadership, has become reflective of (and also productive of) the interesting ferments now taking place in total Christian and Jewish education.

Miller defines the task of Christian education as not so

much teaching theology, but *using* theology as a tool for bringing learners into a right relationship with God through the church. " The clue to Christian education," he writes, " is the rediscovery of a relevant theology which will bridge the gap between content and method, providing the background and perspective of Christian truth by which the best methods and content will be used as tools to bring the learners into the right relationship with the living God who is revealed to us in Jesus Christ, using the guidance of parents and the fellowship of life in the Church as the environment in which Christian nurture will take place." [16]

Other important statements of Miller's that have been widely influential are these: " The center of the curriculum is a twofold relationship between God and the learner. The curriculum is both God-centered and experience-centered. Theology must be prior to the curriculum! Theology is ' truth-about-God-in-relation-to-man.' " [17] " *Theology in the background; faith and grace in the foreground* might well be the slogan for this new point of view." [18]

It is interesting to go through *The Clue to Christian Education* to see how often, and in what ways, Miller uses the " relationship " motif. He uses " relationship " to refer to the relation between man and God and between man and man (" the right relationship with God and [one's] fellows ").[19] He is interested in the " human integration " of a child, which, he says, does not evolve from the child's idea of his parents but from his relationship with them.[20] He sees the act of God and the response of faith made by man as being " in an organic interpersonal relationship which grows out of the educational process but which cannot be guaranteed by it." [21] He points out how a concern for right belief or doctrine can sometimes obscure the primary " personal relationship of Christian faith." " The object of faith is not a concept or a belief or a dogma. Faith for man is man's response to God's faithfulness. It is a personal relationship with man trusting himself to God." [22] Prayer is the channel through which our relationship with God is expressed and strengthened.[23]

Two other books by Randolph Miller followed the *Clue.* The resultant "trilogy" (each book *does* stand alone, however) constitutes a systematic exposition of his total relationship theology as this expresses itself educationally within the church.

In *Biblical Theology and Christian Education* (1956), Miller provides reflections on the bearing of Biblical theology on the task of Christian education at the various age levels. In an early chapter he sets forth his main thesis: that Biblical teaching needs to relate to the understanding of the learner *now.* " As the Bible speaks to them [boys and girls, men and women] within the framework of the Church as a community of the Holy Spirit, the redemptive processes of the Gospel become available to them and the Gospel speaks to them where they are *now.* This is Christian education for the present moment, the point at which God and man enter a renewed personal relationship within a community of persons." [24]

Interestingly, Miller uses also the " old story of salvation " which Sophia Lyon Fahs so forthrightly outlined in order to reject it, as we saw in Chapter 2. Miller also tells it (in Ch. 2 of his book, entitled " The Drama of Redemption "), using, instead of Augustine's seven ages, another, similar scheme derived from Bernhard W. Anderson's *The Unfolding Drama of the Bible.*[25] Miller details the drama of our salvation as if there were five acts in a play: Creation, Covenant, Christ, Church, Consummation [26] — and these acts constitute the outline for his book. In each case he seeks to ascertain what parts of the story can and should be communicated to persons in the different age groups. Unlike Mrs. Fahs's intent, Miller, of course, wants to be able to tell the " old story of salvation " in order to win acceptance for it, but always an acceptance that is relevant to the human situation, remembering his definition of theology as " truth-about-God-in-relation-to-man." The drama is always participated in through the fellowship of persons which the church is: " an experienced relationship with God and man, and it exists wherever the Holy Spirit rules the hearts of men." [27] If, for example, forgiveness is to be taught, its real quality will be communicated only when a congregation is spiritually mature enough to manifest forgiveness in its common life. The forgiveness that God promises must be " evident in the relationships of the congregation," so that " the sinner knows that he is not cast out of the fellowship but that his membership is restored when he is repentant. . . . When this quality of life is evident to those of all ages within the congregation, Christian education takes place, for every member knows that he shares in the Biblical drama of redemption and lives in *Act IV* (Church) of God's mighty acts in history. He knows, furthermore, that *Act V* (Consummation) impinges upon him at every moment." [28]

The ramifications of the life of the church in its bearing on Christian education are explored in the third volume, *Christian Nurture and the Church*. Here he sets forth an understanding of the church much influenced by contemporary accents on the theology of the laity, the meaning of mission, the relation of church to world, the problems of communication within the church, the ecumenical movement.[29]

Miller sees the local church as " the place where we become conscious of the beginning of our Christian nurture " and the total church as the scene wherein Christian character develops. "When we are loyal to God, who works within the fellowship and at the same time stands over it, we have a framework for our loyalty that transcends the immediate cultural situation. Our beliefs guide our actions, and our membership in the group is the channel of grace whereby we are able to approximate God's will for us through our vocation. Ethical behavior is our thanksgiving for God's grace to us through Christ, and by the power of the Spirit we are enabled to fight under God's banner and to continue Christ's faithful servant." [30] The concluding sentence of that quotation, it will be noted, is informed with the words and spirit of the prayer for the confirmand which is spoken by the bishop in *The Book of Common Prayer* of the Protestant Episcopal Church.

Reviewing *Christian Nurture and the Church*, Sara Little, one of his former students at Yale, herself a distinguished theorist, raised the questions as to whether Miller has overemphasized a theology of relationship " at the expense of a theology of confrontation, . . . whether a high enough degree of true Christian community can be achieved to make Christian education a possibility, . . . whether either parish or home in a pluralistic culture like that in contemporary America can overcome the forces with which they are in conflict." [31] The " theology of confrontation " is a phrase that perhaps will take on added scope when we examine it in some detail in the next chapter.

ENTER ENGAGEMENT: *David R. Hunter*

Randolph Crump Miller had served, along with Reuel L. Howe, as a consultant to the Department of Christian Education of the Protestant Episcopal Church during the period when that church was seeking to develop a new curriculum for its Sunday church schools. Something of Howe's psychological concerns and Miller's relationship theology was bound to find its way into the new courses, eventually issued under the designation *The Seabury Series*. The coordinating mastermind for the new curriculum was David R. Hunter. Dr. Hunter had been diocesan director of Christian education for Massachusetts prior to taking his position as executive director of the Department. He also had completed his doctor of education degree at Harvard University, specializing in some aspects of group dynamics studies.

For years Dr. Hunter's friends had been trying to persuade him to produce a book that would set forth his carefully thought through understandings of educational process within the life of the church. Due to the pressures of travel and constant administrative involvement, Hunter was unable to do this until finally he completed a manuscript for the Bradner Lectures, delivered at the Episcopal Theological School, Cambridge. Those lectures constitute Ch. 1 through 5 of *Christian Education as Engagement*, published in 1963.

By "engagement" Hunter means relationship too, but with a somewhat special emphasis. Engagement means meeting and knowing, as differentiated from knowing about something or someone. "*Engagement* is the moment when God acts in or upon the life of an individual and the individual faces the obligation to respond. In as much as God is always acting in all life and upon His entire creation, the whole range of one's experience has this theological dimension of engagement. Moreover, since we know from Christian revelation that all experience of this dimension is made possible by God's grace, then the term, in its Christian context, includes the prior action of being met by, being known, being loved by God." [32] The opposite of engagement is "detachment": "separation from any conscious sense of confronting the living God and dealing with His action in life." [33] Hunter likes to use two other terms with a specialized meaning for him. One is "training." This refers to "being prepared by becoming involved in." The other is "religious issue." He explains the latter: "A religious issue comes into being as a result of a situation where God has acted and man has responded or failed to respond. It is the consequence of engagement and is, therefore, the focus of Christian education." [34]

There are three "inescapable choices" which Christian education must make, Hunter believes. These are: preparing people for the future or ministering to them now where they are; transmitting culture or being a culture-change agent; developing a motivation that is man-dependent (Pelagian) or grace-dependent. The second of each of these alternative choices represents engagement. Likewise, with regard to the methodology of Christian education, engagement will take place only when religious issues become the organizing principle of the curriculum, as against subject matter, which will produce merely detachment. Hunter relates the process to a learning theory embracing four "elements of experience": immediate personal encounter, identification of the encounter, symbolization of the experience, and the ordering of experience.

He concludes: " If we use these four elements of learning in understanding and categorizing the nature of man's response to God, it then becomes possible to say that Christian learning involves an awareness of the action of God within our lives, a recognition of the religious issues which are created by God's action and our response, a relating of this experience and these religious issues to the mighty acts of God in the past, and, finally, some comprehension of the relationship which this past experience or symbol has to the whole body of Christian revelation and Christian experience." [35] He goes on to suggest how the engagement concept pertains to nurture and to mission, giving implications also for day schools under religious auspices and theological education in the seminaries of the church.

What David Hunter does is to extend the concept of engagement to include all that Miller means by relationship and what Sherrill and others mean by encounter, though keeping his focus always very much in terms of the educational process. His understanding of that process is deeply influenced by categories of thinking that spring from group dynamics science: " orientation training," " in-service training," " tactical encounter " and related terms are informed by a group life flavor and bring to mind the processes that Hunter so capably introduced into the Protestant Episcopal Church when the " new " curriculum was inaugurated, such as parish life conferences and group life laboratories. Many of these methods, constituting a genuine innovation in the methodology of religious communication, have been adopted by other denominations and by interdenominational agencies, so that now they are somewhat standard repertoire.

In closing this consideration of the " relationship school " of religious educators, we must add that something of their concern with the dimension of relationship is shared by practically all the thinkers of this period of theological history. They are singled out because they put such a strong accent on this approach that it would seem to be fair to say of them that they are the exponents par excellence of a distinctive relationship-theology motif in contemporary religious education theory.

5

Biblical Bases of Nurture

W HEN the Presbyterian Church in the U.S.A.
(later to become merged with the United Presbyterian Church of North America into The United Presbyterian Church in the U.S.A.) was about to undertake the
enormous task of preparing a new church school curriculum for its parishes, it turned for leadership to a minister
of the Presbyterian Church in Canada, James D. Smart.
He joined the staff of the Board of Christian Education in
1944, spending six years as editor in chief of the emerging
curriculum. It was " new " as a curriculum in more ways
than one. It was the first really revolutionary effort to be
made by any major American denomination in curriculum
production for many years. It was certainly the first one
to be inspired by some of the neoorthodox understandings
of theology.

A NOTE ON NEOORTHODOXY

Before proceeding with a discussion of Dr. Smart's
views, it would be wise, perhaps, to say a few things about
this term " neoorthodoxy." As Roger L. Shinn has suggested, it is possible that the usefulness of this term has

ended, save "as a description of history of the recent past."[1] By this he means that many of its accents were associated with the period from after World War I through World War II and succeeding years, when there was a pronounced reaction, first in Europe, then in America, against many of the tenets of the formerly regnant liberalism. The "neoorthodox" position (stemming from Karl Barth as its intellectual giant) stressed the appeal to Biblical revelation, the transcendence of God, the awareness of human sin, justification by God through Jesus Christ, a recognition of tragedy in history, and a recovery of the eschatological dimension. These, in the view of neoorthodoxy, all were to be seen in sharp focus over against their "contrary" positions, as these had been affirmed by liberalism — the Bible as the record of the human quest for God, the immanence of God, sin seen as ignorance or blindness, justification through good works, history seen as the theater of cosmic progress, the goal of existence conceived in terms of fulfillment on earth.[2] At the same time, while it was insisting on a return to Biblical norms, the neoorthodox movement was quite ready and willing to accept all the findings of the Biblical scholars regarding text and *mythos* — the assured results of historical criticism. This, as we saw in Chapter 1, was one of the baffling things about neoorthodoxy for Harrison S. Elliott, who recognized here a formidable contender for attention by virtue of its intellectual integrity in these respects. By and large, few persons today, either in theologizing proper or in Christian education theorizing, like to be labeled "neoorthodox," yet the term *does* connote a certain stance. It is at least a useful "direction pointer."

THE CHURCH'S TEACHING MINISTRY:

James D. Smart

After being involved in helping to formulate the Presbyterian curriculum along neoorthodox lines, Dr. Smart returned to the pastorate in Toronto, where he also became lecturer in Christian education at Knox College. Pondering upon his recent experiences and his growing convictions about the relation of theology to pedagogy, he set down his ideas in a book, *The Teaching Ministry of the Church*.[3] Its subtitle is " An Examination of the Basic Principles of Christian Education." In his foreword he states that it was his intent not to write from a Presbyterian standpoint only, but rather to take up the " theological bases of Christian education in the most comprehensive sense." To that end he starts with an assumption of validity in the catholic doctrine of the Trinity, showing " the character of the educational program that results when that doctrine is allowed to have its full force in our thinking and in our practices." [4]

Smart rests teaching upon the very foundation of the church itself, insisting that it belongs to the " essence " of the church. Later, J. Stanley Glen, his colleague in Knox College, was to write convincingly of *The Recovery of the Teaching Ministry*,[5] a theme which in a very real sense James Smart first heralded. Smart makes a distinction between preaching and teaching — the former referring to the proclamation of the Word of God " to man in his unbelief," the latter to " the situation of the man who has repented and turned to God and . . . the situation of children of believers who through the influence of their parents have in them a measure of faith, even though they have also in them a large measure of unbelief." [6] He rejects any preaching of the gospel that issues in a moralistic kind of teaching unrelated to the basic *kērygma*. He argues passionately for a recovery of theology as the nexus of the so-called " practical " departments of the life of the church. " The practical considerations are as thoroughly theological as those that arise in the Biblical, systematic, and historical departments of theology. Every theological concern comes here to its practical expression. But it can be understood only when it is traced to its Biblical and theological roots." [7]

He sees the present situation as characterized by a rigidity of tradition (that is, a rigidity stemming from a fixation upon the liberal theology which had so long dominated it), by educational confusion, and by " the suffocating fog of moralism." Character development has replaced salvation as the theme of much education in the church, and the Biblical message has been sold short by inadequate attention to its notes of judgment and grace, while stress has been put on teaching information *about* the Bible rather than the Biblical Word itself.

This is the way he summarizes the rationale for Christian education: " Christian education exists because the life that came into the world in Jesus Christ demands a human channel of communication that it may reach an ever-widening circle of men, women, and children, and become their life. The aim of Christian teaching is to widen and deepen that human channel, to help forward the growth and enrichment of the human fellowship, through which Jesus Christ moves ever afresh into the life of the world to redeem mankind. The program, therefore, must be such that it will lead people, from their earliest to their latest years, ever more fully and in the most definite way into the faith and life of the Church of Jesus Christ." [8]

Dr. Smart devotes chapters to some practical aspects of the Christian education enterprise in the present situation: the nature of religious growth, the place of the home in religious nurture, and the relation of the church to public education. He sees the educational problem, both within the church and within the larger community, as being primarily a theological problem. He thinks it important that the resolution of the theological problem be thoroughly involved in the manner in which the practical problems are regarded and solved. What are some of the "practical" conclusions to which his arguments lead? "They call for reconsideration of the place of Christian education in the theological curriculum and of the place of basic theological disciplines in the curriculum of schools of education. They raise sharply the question of the unity of the ministry, and the right of those who are teachers rather than preachers to share in the full ministry when they are properly trained. They point to the importance of more thorough training in Bible, history, and doctrine for church school teachers. They call for a recognition by the congregation as a whole of its responsibility for teaching. Above all, they set a new aim for education, one that is significant for a Church that is interested in regaining its evangelizing power. The call we hear is simply the call to be the Church for which Jesus Christ lived and died, a royal priesthood, daring to put itself at his service to be used by him for his conquest of the world." [9]

As we read words like those quoted above, we can imagine the kind of reaction they would have produced in adherents of the older school of religious educational liberals. In 1954, when *The Teaching Ministry of the Church* was published, many of them were still occupying positions of influential leadership. His frank espousal of a theological foundation for education in the church brought forth the charge by one reviewer that he was using "that slippery word 'theology' in so many ways that one finds himself having to stop and determine the particular meaning at the moment." The same reviewer said: "The total effect on a general reader may be bad because 'the present situation' is painted in blacks and whites. Actually, though, there has been a great body of religious educators who have sought to keep the program soundly within the framework of the church's organization, thinking, and mission." [10]

Writing from a quite different standpoint, one receptive to the kind of position toward which Smart desired to move the church, Howard Grimes wrote: "At times the author seems to be too little aware of the contributions of progressive education. He would go farther than Miller in his *The Clue to Christian Education,* which has as its thesis that the one thing needed is for progressive educational methods to be undergirded with a sounder theology. This is not to suggest that Smart would have us return to a purely transmissive type of education. He does place more importance on this phase of the educational process, however. Actually, both Smart and Miller ought to be read in order to complement each other, for truly creative education in the Christian faith is not possible without a fairly adequate amount of transmission. One cannot accept for himself the responsibility of discipleship unless he knows the historic meaning of discipleship as discovered through the traditions of the church. Yet to fail to make these traditions existentially relevant is to fall into the trap of mere intellectualism." [11]

It is interesting to note that two of the books we have discussed thus far have grown out of reflections upon the actual involvement of their writers in curricular efforts, and in both cases *after* the completion of their personal service in connection with these programs. David R. Hunter's *Christian Education as Engagement* and James D. Smart's *The Teaching Ministry of the Church* are not merely ivory-tower productions. Each reflects the *Sturm und Drang* of curriculum-making. Back of each we can see the many hours of communal labor, group discussion, staff meetings, field trips, and all the other inevitable accompaniments of this process. In each case, the author has acknowledged this " groupness " which lay back of his production. Hunter writes, " In the development both of the foundations of this program in the Episcopal Church and of the procedures which have been used, the author shares responsibility with scores of colleagues who have worked with him on the national staff and with hundreds of others who have counseled and assisted us in many ways." [12] Soon after writing that, Hunter was to leave his denominational position to become an associate general secretary of the Division of Christian Education of the National Council of the Churches of Christ in the U.S.A. And Smart writes, referring to his colleagues in the Board of Christian Education's editorial staff (Presbyterian, U.S.A.): " So close was our relationship that I can no longer tell what is mine and what is theirs in my understanding of education." [13] Thus we see how individual thinkers both mold and reflect the corporate educational milieu of the churches.

After serving for a number of years in his Toronto parish, Dr. Smart was called to be professor of Biblical interpretation in Union Theological Seminary, New York City. His literary productivity has been turned in the direction of hermeneutics, as evidenced by his *The Interpretation of Scripture*. *The Creed in Christian Teaching* is more a theological than an educational work. *The Rebirth of Ministry* is an examination of the meaning of the Christian concept of ministry in the light of a reevaluation of the Biblical sources and the contemporary reawakening of concern for the place of the laity in ministry.[14]

AN EXISTENTIAL DYNAMIC FOR EDUCATION:
Iris V. Cully

With Iris V. Cully a new note entered the developing reconstruction of Christian education theory: the existentialist dimension. Before we enter upon a discussion of her approach, it would seem desirable to pause briefly for a short discourse on the meaning of existentialism. Those who already have read widely in contemporary philosophy, theology, and especially in belles-lettres of the avant-guarde variety will not need this detour.

Existentialism is best thought of as a point of view, a "posture" (i.e., position), to use Roger Shinn's phrase. George F. Kneller describes it as "an intellectual revolt against the systematization of man by science, philosophy, and religion," declaring that "philosophy should express the concrete and total life experience of the individual rather than the abstract view of universal reason."[15]

The existentialist does not think that one can frame a "system" of any kind that can embalm truth. He puts an emphasis on involvement, decision, particular situations, the "leap" of faith. There are actually two streams of existentialist thought — one quite definitely "secular," even atheistic in its orientation; the other, springing from Søren Kierkegaard, deeply religious. In recent decades the field of theology has been much influenced by this type of approach, especially in the writings of such persons as Gabriel Marcel, Nicolas Berdyaev, and the early Karl Barth. Referring to this influence of existentialism in theological thought, George Kneller writes: "The Christian educator . . . will have to strike a balance between the existentialist's hostility to doctrinal systems and the claims of a more orthodox theology." [16]

Whether there is any inevitable hostility between doctrinal systems and the existentialist position is debatable. Surely the existentialist would avoid all semblance of finality with regard to any statement *about* theological presuppositions, but he would take seriously the demands *of* such doctrines for actual living.

In a sense Iris V. Cully sought in her book *The Dynamics of Christian Education* to bring classical theological understandings into full view and then to ask whether these do not in themselves suggest, by their embodiment of the dynamic of Christian faith itself, certain things about the church's teaching task.[17] She starts with a Biblically-oriented neoorthodoxy but finds this position leading to a deeply life-centered understanding of educational methodology.

Iris Virginia (Arnold) Cully was born in New York City and as a small child attended a Methodist church, though during her secondary school years she was confirmed in the Reformed Church in America. After graduating from Adelphi College, she took her master of arts degree in the Hartford Seminary Foundation, studying with such leaders in liberal religious education as

A. J. William Myers. For a brief time before her marriage she was director of Christian education in a Presbyterian parish in Hollis, New York. Married to a clergyman (a Congregationalist who later became an Episcopalian), she has been actively involved in varied parish and denominational programs, though she always continued to make religious education matters her chief focus of interest. She was invited to write curriculum materials for several denominations, including the Presbyterian Church in the U.S.A. (having been one of the first group of writers for their *Christian Faith and Life* curriculum), the Congregational Christian Churches, and the Evangelical and Reformed Church (now the United Church of Christ). After she and her husband moved with their two daughters to Evanston, Illinois, she resumed theological studies, completing the bachelor of divinity degree at Garrett Theological Seminary and the doctor of philosophy degree at Northwestern University. She has been a visiting lecturer in Christian education or religion at Garrett, Northwestern, Lutheran School of Theology (Chicago), Pacific School of Religion, Union Theological Seminary (New York), Yale University, New York University, and Drew University.

Her personal ecclesiastical background, involving exposure to several traditions, and her spectrum of studies, have led her into what she deems " an appreciable consensus . . . among the exponents of what might be termed an ecumenical theology." It is against this background that she writes in *The Dynamics of Christian Education:* " Those persons responsible for Christian nurture are showing concern that children's lives shall be rooted in the fellowship of the church, that their faith shall be awakened by the hearing of the gospel, and that their lives shall be guided by the work of the Holy Spirit. For these reasons contemporary understandings in Biblical study and in Biblical theology are finding a response among workers in the field of religious education. Many are seeking ways by which understandings of the Christian faith that have been meaningful to believers since the earliest days of the church can be meaningful in the lives of growing persons now." [18]

Dr. Cully differentiates between the cultural school and the church school, suggesting that these are " two communities " that " exist together within the same geographical milieu." She writes: " Everyone belongs to the cultural community. Some belong to the community of the church. . . . By understanding the purposes of cultural education, persons within the church are enabled more clearly to apprehend the unique and particular function that is given the Christian community." There are, however, potential points of conflict also. " This is implicit in asserting that the democratic ideal is the ultimate form of corporate existence, or that men are inherently good; that scientific method is the only respectable form of teaching; or that all problems can be solved intellectually. . . . Those persons who are concerned with Christian nurture need to realize these pressures, for they affect the approach to be used in communicating the faith." [19]

She then goes on to interpret the church as the context of Christian education, and the *kērygma* as the very heart of the Christian faith — the saving activity of God as it is recorded in the Bible and preached in the apostolic witness of the early church. In her discussion of " The Content of Christian Education," Dr. Cully presents the classical account of the divine-human encounter as it is generally seen within the contemporary theological discussions informed by the Biblical theology.

But at this point she thinks it necessary — indeed, mandatory — to turn to " the persons to whom the good news is to be addressed." [20] An entire chapter in the *Dynamics* is thus devoted to a consideration of " Persons and Communication." Here we see how she uses something of an existential position, tracing the expression of it in contemporary drama, poetry, psychology, and sociology. God's revelation is to human beings in their actual condition and situation, not in terms of some abstract propositionalism. " Since God is personal, knowledge of him must be in personal terms and must come from him. Man does not ' discover ' God, although he may discover objective facts about God. . . . The knowledge of God comes only by the gracious action of God himself as he seeks to make himself known to his children in love." [21] Man's response to revelation she calls " appropriation."

In outlining a theory of methodology, she proceeds from the *kērygma* to the *didachē.* The proclamation takes place not only through formal preaching, but through confessions of faith (creeds), hymnody, the Sacraments, and *caritas* (Christian charity). The whole teaching task of the church is dependent on the *kērygma.* " The content of the church's teaching is found in the basic message of the early church, the *kērygma,* and the resultant forms of teaching, the *didachē.* . . . The ' what ' of Christian nurture is so to make known the *kērygma* that growing children may respond to God's saving love made known in Christ and live in relationship with him, committing their lives to him and finding the gift of the Holy Spirit through the life of the church to empower them in their every relationship." [22]

The " how " consists of life-centered methods capable of

conveying the dynamic *kērygma*. Iris Cully uses "life-centered" differently from the way in which it was used under the pragmatic religious education philosophies. "It usually has meant 'experience-centered,' and this reference has connoted present experience. The result was an intense interest in the moment and clear plans for the future, but only a fragmentary view of the past, which was construed as usable primarily in order to enrich the present." She prefers an interpretation of "life-centered" which takes into account the deeper levels of "life" as enunciated by the existentialist theologians and philosophers. Existence rather than abstract being is the focus. "Existence comprises a totality — not the self by itself, but the self in relationship to others, things, the universe, and history." [23]

This existential involvement is interpreted by Dr. Cully in terms of three categories, which constitute her methodological types. The first is *participation*. By this she does not mean merely "personal participation in a present group situation." Rather, "there is a further level in participation in which the self apprehends the persons with whom he participates; and beyond that there is the ability to participate with persons in historic events." [24] Historical remembrance — "re-presentation" — is involved here as well as "a child's participation through present experience." "When he [the pupil] can see his needs and problems against those of Biblical persons, he has a focus beyond himself from which to view himself." This is not to be confused with "the psychologizing of Bible stories," a tendency which she repudiates, "but only to indicate that they show a penetrating understanding of the dynamics of human need and response. . . . The learner is not alone. Others have felt this way. God who saved then can save now. The child is surrounded by a company of believers, the fellowship of those who have been called, the body of whom Christ is the head and which is indwelt by the Holy Spirit." [25] A similar existential involvement through participation can be achieved through the arts, especially painting, music, drama, poetry, and story.

The child's experience is deepened as he is enabled to see it in the broader context which art discloses. He participates with the artist, who also has participated in the past, both in the message that he remembers and in the forms and technique for composition that are the bases for his art. Each century produces art that is the expression of its existence, yet each builds on the forms that were given by previous centuries. This too is remembrance. But in Christian art, the form is used for the expression of a particular content: the gospel, the proclamation of God's saving work for men through Jesus Christ.[26]

Iris Cully calls stage two in her statement of methodology *recognition*. " Participation is a form of learning open to even the smallest child. Recognition is an awareness that comes through participation, but which is a personal response on the part of the learner." [27] This stage of methodology is akin to the I-Thou encounter of which Buber speaks; it is related to " insight." Its means are prayer and worship especially. It is the stage of learning in which through faith one appropriates faith and accepts responsibility before God. " When encounter has been followed by response, the child willingly becomes a part of the Christian community." [28]

Stage three is called *communication*. " Participation leads to recognition. Recognition seeks a way of expression. The expression is communication." [29] This is not merely " the sharing of ideas "; nonverbal means, such as symbols, can be involved as well. Pupils communicate with one another through conversation, discussion, witnessing, questioning, and — in the classroom — through such devices as personal composition (words, music, painting, etc.) through which they express their understanding to one another. The ways of communication become enhanced through the children's growing self-knowledge which can provide the basis for self-transcendence. This is to be differentiated from " independence "; it is " the voluntary dependence of one who accepts a relationship in love and [who] begins to be aware of the fact that love is a paradoxical situation: it is a joyful bondage which gives the kind of freedom that can come only from that kind of security." She summarizes her methodology thus: " Participation can be understood now, for it is entered into voluntarily. Recognition is made complete, for it is done in full knowledge of the self. Communication can be clear, for the person knows himself in relation to time and space, to the world and other persons, and to God who is the source of his life and his Redeemer." [30]

In her last chapter, " Focus for the Future," Dr. Cully analyzes the implications of the *kērygma-didachē* relationship for curriculum in the light of her suggested methodology. New understandings, she suggests, need to be forthcoming in curriculum for the church, especially in regard to the use of the Bible, the relationship between God and man, and the nature of human conduct. Her book *The Dynamics of Christian Education* ends with the argument that the dynamic Biblical theology presently understood within the church needs to be presented through dynamic, existential teaching methods. The methods used must be consonant with a methodology arising from the dynamic of the Christian gospel itself.[31]

In later works Iris Cully has explored two aspects of her

basic position in relation to the place of children in the life of the church and the role of the Bible in Christian education. Like Lewis Sherrill's *The Gift of Power,* her *Children in the Church* was a selection of the Pastoral Psychology Book Club and consequently found its way into large numbers of clergy libraries.[32] In the *Preview* of that book club, she wrote on her purpose in writing the book:

Each year when I give the course on " The Church's Ministry to Children," I find that there are more and more pastors, as well as student pastors, who are eager to know more about children and the ways in which to work with children in the church. I have observed that alert clergymen long since out of seminary also have a conscientious interest in becoming more aware of recent developments in the understanding of the child as these pertain to their younger parishioners.

This book was developed to meet the needs of persons like these students and pastors. It seeks to provide up-to-date information about children in relation to their physical needs, their developmental tasks, and their religious growth. . . . The core of the book lies in the chapters describing methods through which Christian nurture brings the child to the decision by which he enters full, participating membership in the church . . . (and) the discussion of ways by which the child is helped to witness to his own faith and to communicate his understandings to others by word and deed.[33]

Imparting the Word: The Bible in Christian Education [34] (1962) sets forth a rationale for the understanding and use of the Bible in Christian education. Dr. Cully states: " The Bible is a central source in Christian education because the basic purposes cannot be realized except through an understanding of its contents. God makes himself known through this written word. The church finds its foundations in this word. The Christian knows the wellsprings for his actions to be sustained here." [35] She seeks to interpret the place of the Bible in terms of the purposes of Christian education, which she has defined (as a possible way of stating what can be variously put) " to help people through their growing relationship to God in Christ so to live that they may glorify him and effectively serve others, in the assurance that they partake of eternal life now and forever." The book summarizes some of the findings of contemporary Biblical scholarship, pointing out their implications — seldom recognized heretofore in the church's program of nurture — for the educational task, including a frank facing of the mythological element in Scripture and the use of the Bible in the liturgy of the church.[36]

FOUNDATIONS FOR CURRICULUM:
D. Campbell Wyckoff

Another writer with a neoorthodox, Biblically-based approach is D. Campbell Wyckoff. Dr. Wyckoff, a United Presbyterian layman, taught religious education in New York University for some years before being called to the faculty of Princeton Theological Seminary, where he has been Thomas W. Synnott Professor of Christian Education since 1954, and in addition, more recently, director of doctoral studies.

In 1955, Dr. Wyckoff entered into the process of the theological reevaluation of religious nurture by writing *The Task of Christian Education*. In his Preface he describes the way in which his book was developed. He related his message to actual groups of church people to whom he was asked to speak from time to time — parents, teachers, leadership training classes, pastors, as well as his regular classes at New York University. Later, transcriptions of these various presentations were made, and the final text emerged as edited material from these real-life situations. Thus he was motivated from the beginning to direct his thinking along lines that would be helpful to those who were engaged in the operational aspects of the church's educational program.

Wyckoff sets forth a definition of religious education as " the guided process of helping growing persons to achieve at each stage of their growth such habits, skills, attitudes, appreciations, knowledges, ideas, ideals, and intentions as will enable them at each stage to achieve an ever more integrated personality, competent and satisfying living in their social environment, and increasing co-operativeness with God and man in the reconstruction of society into a fellowship of persons." [37] He attributes this definition to the late Samuel L. Hamilton, his predecessor at New York University, and suggests that as a working definition this process can be adapted to " a Christian interpretation of the nature of God and his will, and an understanding and practice of the reality of Christ in the life of man." What he proceeds to do in his book is to give the Christian interpretation of Hamilton's definition, which could as well, he suggests, be applied to faiths other than Christian. It will be seen that Wyckoff sought to move from the earlier concerns with generalized definitions of *religious* education aims into more specifically *Christian* understandings. He sets forth the following as the aim of Christian education: " to nurture the Christian life." Such nurture, he says, involves Christian instruction, the redemption of the individual, and the redemption of society.[38] His neo-orthodox orientation is manifested in such a statement as this: " The Christian discovers in the process of search a truth he possibly has not foreseen: that the Christian life is not properly man's search for God at all. The Christian life is more properly God's search for man. The objects of the search — truth, righteousness, and the good life — become clearer when we realize that it is God who is searching for us." [39]

In 1959, Dr. Wyckoff wrote *The Gospel and Christian Education: A Theory of Christian Education for Our Times* as an effort to establish some guideposts toward " building a theory of Christian education " on the basis of " principles that will give Protestants a clear idea of what Christian education is concerned with, and will provide the guidance needed for the practical aspects of the church's work in objectives, curriculum, and administration." He sought a body of principles that could be " theologically valid and educationally sound." [40] As an organizing principle for the curriculum he suggests the gospel itself: " God's redeeming activity in Jesus Christ," which he sees as containing the clue to the meaning of existence, history, and the church. It is also " the clue to human becoming." He states the guiding principle thus: " If Christian education will focus its attention on the gospel, it will be properly oriented and conceived. Around the gospel the other elements of Christian education may be grouped, but it is the one element that can stand alone and give the others meaning. The gospel is the essential element in establishing the institutions of Christian education and devising their curriculums." [41]

Subsequently Dr. Wyckoff issued *Theory and Design of Christian Education Curriculum,* which has established itself as the principal book on the theory of Protestant curriculum, a long-overdue successor to earlier works by Betts and Bower, which had appeared in the 1920's. [42] This volume reflected his continuous and intimate involvement in consultations on objectives and curriculum held under the aegis of the National Council of the Churches of Christ in the U.S.A. He defines a theory of curriculum that will pay adequate attention to context, scope, purpose, process, and design. He construes theology as being properly used in an effort to determine these aspects of the curriculum procedures, as well as being an ingredient that should enter into the actual teaching materials. He sees a place for the inclusion of both " the language of relationships and the spoken language."

Christian education deals with the vocabulary of the gospel and the Word of God. The Word of God is his way of revealing himself to us. It has been a spoken word; it is the word made flesh in Jesus Christ; it is the written word, the Bible, witnessed to by the Holy Spirit. God's own language is quite clearly a combination of the spoken and the unspoken, the verbal and the nonverbal, a language of words and a language of relationships: he acts, he talks, he shows, he sends, he waits; he enters, he heals, he teaches, he preaches, he prays; he suffers, he dies, he rises, he ascends, he lives and reigns; he returns; and through it all he creates, he loves, and he redeems.

Our challenge is to be able to speak in lives and at the same time in words that learners can understand accurately, that can get through to them, making things clear to them, and helping them in turn to be able to speak a language that expresses their faith and life.[48]

6

Fundamentalism
and Neo-evangelicalism

SOMETHING of the attitudes and presuppositions of the traditional Christian denominations against which the liberal movement (and hence its religious education) was a protest has continued in some Christian circles. This constitutes an insistence on certain doctrinal views based strictly on what is frequently called "Biblical truth." In 1943, for example, the National Association of Evangelicals adopted a "doctrinal statement" which reads as follows:

We believe the Bible to be the inspired, the only infallible, authoritative Word of God. We believe that there is one God, eternally existent in three Persons, Father, Son, and Holy Ghost. We believe in the deity of our Lord Jesus Christ, in his virgin birth, in his sinless life, in his miracles, in his vicarious and atoning death through his shed blood, in his bodily resurrection, in his ascension to the right hand of the Father, and in his personal return in power and glory. We believe that for the salvation of lost and sinful man regeneration by the Holy Spirit is absolutely essential. We believe in the present ministry of the Holy Spirit by whose indwelling the Christian is enabled to live a godly life. We believe in the resurrection of both the saved and the lost; they that are saved unto the resurrection of life and they that are lost unto the resurrection of damnation. We believe in the spiritual unity of believers in our Lord Jesus Christ.[1]

This organization grew out of a protest against some of the theological and social concerns of the former Federal Council of the Churches of Christ in America (now the National Council), and to a certain extent its affirmation of a creedal position must be construed as arising from an effort to state the differences between "fundamentalists" and "modernists." (The Association was founded in 1942 before the strong entry of neoorthodox thinking into the front ranks of American church leadership.)

The term "fundamentalist" grew out of a series of booklets widely circulated from 1909 on, entitled *The Fundamentals*. These pamphlets dealt with an exposition of traditional "orthodox" positions in theology, such as atonement through propitiation, the reality of hell, and the Second Coming of Christ. Some of them were efforts to refute the allegations of Biblical criticism, which had come to dominate the liberalist movement, in terms of a doctrine of inspiration. Some attacked evolutionary views and other theories from science which seemed to denigrate "orthodox" Christianity. Gabriel Hebert summarizes these papers: "There are clearly two strands; one is the 'battle royal for the fundamentals,' for the Gospel of God itself, and the other is the rejection of scientific and critical-historical theories which appeared to be inconsistent with faith in God's revelation." The liberal theologians seemed to these writers "to be betraying that Faith of which they were accredited teachers, and endorsing the suspicion in the popular mind that the Bible was 'a fallen oracle.'"[2]

Depending on the critic's perspective, fundamentalists have been regarded as vigilant and aggressive defenders of orthodox faith, on the one hand, or, on the other hand, as extremists and individualists more interested in maintaining little splinter groups of Christians than in addressing the colossal problems facing Christendom in the encounter with the modern world.

An early fundamentalist writer asserted: "Many modern critics are blameworthy for failing to distinguish within fundamentalism between the solid core of biblical Christianity and certain excrescences; fundamentalists have often contributed to the judgment that it is essentially a religious novelty." He points to "the presence at times of a zeal not according to knowledge and the frequent absence of historical perspective and the appreciation of scholarship" as well as "pietistic and perfectionist 'vagaries'" and "a one-sided otherworldliness, often associated with a dogmatic commitment to a futuristic chiliasm" as some characteristics that led many to reject the fundamentalist witness.[3]

Carl F. H. Henry, editor of *Christianity Today* and a leading neo-evangelical scholar, points to the difference between some naïve types of fundamentalism and the nascent new form of evangelicalism of which he himself is an articulate exponent. He cites the fact that fundamentalist schools became anti-intellectualistic in tone in the days after the first glow of the fundamentalist reaction to liberalism had faded. "Furthermore, first-rate evangelical scholars were increasingly at a premium; for more than a generation it had been popular to defect to the modernist forces. While evangelicals took some active part in the theological debate, they tended to reactionary positions in maintaining the defenses, and were prone to excessive formulations of convictions. . . . Evangelical polemics became largely negative, and sought primarily the approbation of its own conservative constituency rather than the effective penetration of competing spheres of influence."

Dr. Henry goes on to say that the newer evangelical scholars are avoiding "these reactionary defenses of the past," being cognizant of "the high view as over against the classic liberal repudiation and the neo-orthodox evasion of scriptural inspiration." [4] In other words, he seems to be urging a type of fundamentalist thought that would be intellectually advanced, attractively presented, and intelligently defended. One might, therefore, differentiate between a traditionalist fundamentalism and a more sophisticated neo-evangelicalism, though, stated thus, the differentiation might be rejected by many who would insist that the aim of all evangelicals is to defend Biblical truth, and that alone. But the defense, of course, is in terms of the presuppositions whereby "Biblical truth" is defined.

Conceivably, if one were to be very careful in defining the subtleties of the distinctions among various types of fundamentalist thinkers, one might come up with four groups: anti-intellectualistic fundamentalists; intellectually-oriented fundamentalists ("conservatives"); evangelicals (fundamentalists who are intellectually oriented but desire to stress the evangelistic enterprise of the Christian witness); neo-evangelicals (intellectuals who put a stress on rationalistic doctrine but still espouse a strong evangelistic concern — evangelistic academicians, as it were). Actually, such a classification is at best artificial. The fact is that a fundamentalistic attitude exists within most of the main-line church bodies as a small minority and outside the mainstream churches in autonomous denominations pledged to various types of orthodoxies. [5] Regional and sociocultural aspects enter into any such discussion as well as strictly theological factors. These non-theological factors, in the long run, may indeed be more determinative of the complexion of American church life than we usually recognize.

The fundamentalistically inclined denominations and individual churches within the mainstream denominations who espouse a " conservative " view in spite of the general position of their denominations are educationally dependent upon various "nondenominational" agencies or publishers. These publishers provide curriculum materials for the Sunday church school and other institutions of education. Usually they find a common ground in what is sometimes called a " Bibliocentric " view. That phrase, indeed, is the subtitle of one of the standard textbooks on fundamentalist education used in some of the Bible colleges.[6]

In some cases the Bible is claimed to be the center of the curriculum, partly in order to avoid problems presented by the nice distinctions in theological emphasis which sometimes exist among the denominational groups to which these publishers are suppliers. One well-known publisher whose materials are now produced under a private, nonprofit foundation seeks to adhere to a strictly narrative rendition of actual Biblical materials, without editorial comment or interpretation whatsoever. This, it is assumed, gives the local church liberty to use the material in whatever theological focus it desires. Baptism as a Sacrament could be treated under such an approach only with the greatest difficulty, since no explanation of baptism with reference to infants, for example, could be introduced, even assuming, as most churches do, that the baptism of whole households would have included the youngest members of the family. Such an interpretation could afford offense to adherents of believer's baptism only, so it must be omitted, according to such a viewpoint.

Two writers have had considerable influence in the educational circles of fundamentalism and neo-evangelicalism. Their influence is somewhat interchangeable, though Lois E. LeBar is more popular in strict fundamentalist circles and Frank E. Gaebelein tends to be identified with the "neo-evangelical" groups.

CHRIST THE CENTER: *Lois E. LeBar*

Lois E. LeBar has been professor of Christian education and chairman of the graduate department in that field in Wheaton College, Illinois, for many years. Prior to teaching there, she did graduate work in New York University, where she took her doctor of philosophy degree. She has been actively engaged in Sunday church school work in the wide variety of evangelistic church activity centered in Wheaton.

Dr. LeBar desires to pursue an education that is completely Christ-centered. "The power and the presence of Christ himself are to attend our teaching of all nations," she writes, in reference to the Great Commission (Matt. 28:19-20). "His presence and power give Christian teaching its distinctiveness, its transcendent quality that lifts it above the secular level. When Christian teachers observe all things that Christ has commanded and are full to overflowing with the Life and the Word of God, the Life of Christ in them begets Life. Then the Spirit of God uses the truths of the written Word to make Christ near and real to his individual pupil." Such is the general theme of her 1958 book, *Education That Is Christian.*[7]

She regrets that Christians have been contented to borrow "man-made systems of education" instead of building a system based on the central place of the Word of God. On the other hand, Dr. LeBar cautions against confusing preaching and teaching. By this she means that too many lay teachers think of their task as doing somewhat the same thing the preacher does in his pulpit. " The peculiar genius of teaching is the small intimate group in which overt interaction is possible." [8]

Although she argues for a " distinctive " education for Christianity, she is quite willing to borrow some insights from the secular educational theorists, insofar as these seem relevant to the spiritual teaching task. She especially likes the way in which John Amos Comenius balanced " inner and outer factors " in his didactic approach: content *and* pupil concern. She thinks that one can find clues to an educational methodology from the Bible itself and she offers a number of illustrations of Jesus' teaching methods. [9]

As might be expected, granted her presuppositions, the use of the Bible in teaching is of great concern to Lois LeBar. She laments the fact that evangelicals have " staunchly defended the verbal inspiration of the Scriptures and the infallibility of our authority against those who would judge the Word of God rather than letting it judge them," but at the same time neglected the *use* of the Bible on a high enough level. She says that many teachers use the Bible at the level of " Bible baseball games," never getting beyond verbal repetition. " When unreal words are added to unreal words, the whole process is founded upon unreality." Pupils fail to be taught in such a way as to have their attention directed to " the relevance of the doctrine to life." " They have seldom met the Living Word through the written Word." [10]

As a goal of the teaching-learning process, Dr. LeBar

offers the concept of "productive Christian personality."
She lists eight steps or means whereby any Christian can
"improve" personal productivity if he takes pains to observe them: (1) Let the Word of Christ dwell in us richly
in all wisdom; (2) let the Spirit of God free us from the
flesh, which is constantly clamoring to intrude into spiritual activities; (3) give the Lord a chance to lead in any
direction by not shutting off possibilities consonant with
Scripture; (4) keep motivation strong and pure; (5) keep
problems sharply focused; (6) seek the depths of problems and acquire thorough orientation; (7) use perspira-
tion as well as inspiration; (8) be yielded and courageous,
alert and relaxed.[11]

In a final chapter, Dr. LeBar writes of "The Human
Teacher Working with the Divine Teacher." In a section
entitled "The Holy Spirit in the Teacher Himself," [12] she
makes the following observations: "(1) The Holy Spirit
seeks to become our life, deeper than thought or feeling;
(2) the Spirit works through the written Word to exalt
the living Christ of the cross; (3) the only work that
counts is His work through us; (4) our part is to be ready
to receive the divine guidance and power that the Spirit
comes to give; (5) we must practice active submission to
the Holy Spirit and be passive toward the strivings of the
self-life."

It will be observed from the above lists that something
of a moral effort is commended to the Christian as a goal
to strive for, though in the second list (the one referring
to the Holy Spirit) she takes pains to insist that "the only
work that counts is His work through us." The emphasis
on the Holy Spirit is in terms of an individual's subjective
relationship with the Spirit in contrast to the corporate
emphasis which the more churchly oriented approaches

would make. Likewise, it seems to be assumed throughout her book that the Bible as the Word of God will be self-evident to the student through diligent application to the Biblical text. The teacher's task, therefore, would seem to be becoming an instrument of the Holy Spirit. "Without making Himself conspicuous," she writes, "the third member of the Trinity acts as Expediter to remove obstructions so that both the written and Living Word may have free course in the life. The human teacher is merely a humble apprentice for the divine Executive, an understudy who likewise seeks to get the pupil interacting with the Word." [13]

Methodologically speaking, Dr. LeBar accepts quite readily the usual tested approaches from secular sources. In actual practice much fundamentalist teaching tends to put an accent on methods that tend to transmit content rather than to stimulate existential questions, as, for example, the neoorthodox Biblically-oriented theorists would recommend. Thus we find considerable emphasis on mnemonic devices, finger plays, memorization of Bible verses, and songs (such as so-called "choruses") with what seem to be moralistically-oriented themes. The traditional Herbartian method of lesson development, which once dominated most American Sunday school curriculum, has tended to last longer in fundamentalist circles than elsewhere, though certainly Dr. LeBar repudiates the Herbartian in favor of a Comenian approach.[14]

THE INTEGRATION OF TRUTH:
Frank E. Gaebelein

When Frank E. Gaebelein retired as headmaster of the Stony Brook School (Long Island, New York), he did not opt for seclusion but chose to take on a new dimension of an already productive career. He joined Carl F. H. Henry on the editorial staff of the journal *Christianity Today*, an acknowledged neo-evangelical mouthpiece, comparable to *The Christian Century*, which has had a long and distinguished career as the leading nondenominational (now self-styled "ecumenical") paper of opinion and news. Dr. Gaebelein has demonstrated his literary capacities in a number of books, critical articles, and reviews. He graduated from New York University and took an A.M. degree at Harvard University. He holds honorary doctorates from the seminary of the Reformed Episcopal Church, in which he is a minister, and from Wheaton College.

When the National Association of Evangelicals met at Minneapolis in 1946, it established a committee whose assignment was to draw up a comprehensive statement on the philosophy and practice of Christian education. Dr. Gaebelein was elected chairman of that committee, whose work was eventually published in 1951 under the title *Christian Education in a Democracy*.[15] This was not so much a committee's "groupthink" production as it was Dr. Gaebelein's rewriting and reshaping of the conclusions reached by the committee in its intensive deliberations. In this sense it is reminiscent of Paul H. Vieth's editorship of *The Church and Christian Education*,[16] which emerged in 1947 from a similar study commission of the National Council of the Churches of Christ in the U.S.A. (Parenthetically, it is interesting to observe the almost universal "separate but equal" parallelisms between the fundamentalist groups and the mainstream churches. In addition to these two parallel reports, there are the two councils, previously noted. The work *Religious*

Education: A Comprehensive Survey, edited by Marvin J. Taylor, was followed by *An Introduction to Evangelical Christian Education,* edited by J. Edward Hakes, both works covering, from different perspectives, similar spectra of materials and ideas. There are doubtless other parallelisms.) [17]

Against the background of the American situation with regard to the separation of church and state, the report written by Dr. Gaebelein asks: "Why have our schools failed in the development of moral character? They have failed because there has been ruled out of them the only dynamic able to produce character tough enough to weather an ethical climate where the winds blow in the direction of moral short cuts and easy self-indulgence. From trying to 'make God an elective subject,' public education has now been brought to the pass of refusing to give God even so much as elective status. All this has been done in the name of the essential principle of separation of Church and State and in behalf of freedom from authoritarianism. The result is that the Bible, the greatest moral and spiritual source book in the world, has no place on the required reading list of our American youth." [18]

The committee presents what it considers to be a manifesto rather than "a mere dispassionate survey." "Like all Christian witness, it seeks a verdict." [19] What is the kind of education that Christianity must insist upon? The answer is given in terms of knowledge — teaching the kind of knowledge that is "relevant to education and at the same time true to Biblical categories." That which distinguishes a Christian philosophy of education from other positions is "this one thing — the centrality of Jesus Christ. . . . He is the goal of philosophy, for He is Himself that truth and final reality which philosophy seeks."

The educational process consists of " (1) the recipients of education, the pupils; (2) the eternal Administrator, who is also the Father of the pupils; (3) the divine Teacher who is also Redeemer; (4) the living knowledge taught and its outcome." [20]

Actually, the centrality of Jesus Christ is later interpreted in such a way as to subsume Jesus the revealer under the category of the Bible; thus: " The answer to the question, ' Upon what foundations? ' may be summarized in a few words: simply stated, it is the Bible with its life-giving revelation of Jesus Christ. But let us not be deceived by this seeming simplicity. To comprehend the message of the Bible is to think the thoughts of God; to experience Jesus Christ is to experience eternal reality. And to do these things, even within the bounds of finite intelligence, is to have found the integrating factor not just of an educational philosophy but of the whole of life itself." [21]

The study continues with a discussion of the nature of Christian schools on the secondary and collegiate level as well as the Bible colleges and institutes, which are labeled " a new form of American education." [22] There is also a discussion of the qualities desirable in a Christian teacher, the principles that should underlie the Christian Sunday school, the strategic role of the home in religious nurture. A chapter entitled " This Then Is Christian Youth " describes the qualities which hopefully will result from fidelity to the evangelical principles of education: youth will be personally committed to Christ in the whole person; they will have " profound convictions regarding the organic unity of the universe of God's creation "; they will not be naïve, but fully panoplied to battle against the secular foes arrayed against faith; their life " will manifest the indispensable virtue of hard work "; they will exhibit "spiritual discernment"; they will show "obedience to God" in all the situations of life. "And so the portrait of Christian youth differs not only in degree but also in kind from the likeness of secular youth. His eyes are open to something to which the secular mind is blind — that values are expressions of the holy will of an infinite God." [23]

In the above "portrait" some of the characteristic emphases of evangelical education are spelled out clearly in relation to the desired goals of this education. The aim is to achieve a "radical difference between the product of Christian education and that of the world." This reflects the world-renouncing aspects of some evangelical (or ascetic) thought, appearing in church life from the early church onward. [24] The result of this theme has sometimes been, in the past, a neglect of social issues. Dr. Gaebelein discusses this frankly, showing that in some evangelical circles "a test of orthodoxy . . . was for the pulpit to ignore discussion of such themes, the result being almost a smothering of the responsibility of the ministry to deal with social problems." [25] He is referring, of course, to the tendency for an extreme "rightist" political position to have a considerable influence on fundamentalist church opinions, in some places, as represented in the organized opposition to the National Council of the Churches of Christ in the U.S.A. on the ground that it has been allegedly infiltrated with "leftist" views. Such charges often have emanated from leadership synonymous with the leadership in some of the "conservative" church bodies.

This neglect of social concern is here repudiated. "Christian education, backed by more consistent adult example, is obligated to do more than it has yet done in showing youth that the Bible has a great deal to say about injustice, hatred, civic corruption, and all the other evils of our day. It needs to recover the second aspect of the prophetic office, that of forthtelling. . . . While never losing sight of the fact that men and women must first of all know Christ and His salvation, it must be made to see that nothing which causes human anguish is alien to the Saviour." [26] The awareness of the socially prophetic ministry is recognized here. The question, some might say, remains whether this " evil " is still conceived by neo-evangelicals in terms of something Christians can battle against in solitary fashion, and whether they really have come to grips with the evil written into the very social structures themselves, requiring corporate witness and action if they are to be confronted by Christians in the name of the Lord.

The question of " integration " of the Biblical truth with secular learning is one that has been of major interest to Dr. Gaebelein. In *The Pattern of God's Truth* (1954), he deals extensively with this matter. In fact, it might be said that this is the theme of the entire volume, whose subtitle is: " Problems of Integration in Christian Education." The author calls it " in the nature of a supplement to . . . *Christian Education in a Democracy*." [27] The chapters of this book were delivered as the Griffith Thomas Memorial Lectures for 1953 at the Conservative Baptist Theological Seminary of Denver as the Lectures on Christian Thought and Ministry.

Dr. Gaebelein refers to the " external " and " internal " meanings of Christian education. By " external " he means the reference of Christian education to the teaching of God's truth, which, " whether or not we know it or understand it, believe it, or teach it . . . remains his truth." " As for the internal meaning of Christian education, it is something quite different. It relates to the inner workings

of education, to all of its courses and every one of its pol-
icies. And in addition it also has to do with the integration of these things with its external meaning."

He explains further what he means by this problem of
integration:

On the one hand, God's truth is external to Christian education in that it is not dependent upon what education is or does.
On the other hand, there is, as integration proceeds, a merging
of the internal into the external. Thus the internal, though always subordinate to the external, joins in living union with the
external, which remains transcendently beyond it. This is the
heart of integration and the crux of the matter.

Thus integration is " the living union of its subject matter,
administration, and even of its personnel, with the eternal
and infinite pattern of God's truth." [28]

It will be noted that this concept of " integration " is
not the same as " dialogue " in the Buberian sense, or " engagement " as Hunter has used that term. There is an objective " givenness " about God's truth which is not subject to scrutiny, as other kinds of truth might be. The aim
is not so much to bring the gospel into dialogue with man's
views and situations as to arrange for the integration of
all secular truth into God's truth. Gaebelein insists that
truth is one — that anything true belongs to God and is
of God. Thus he writes: " This comprehensive fact of all
truth being God's truth breaks down, on the one hand,
the division of knowledge between secular and religious;
and brings, on the other hand, every area of life and
thought ' into captivity to the obedience of Christ,' to use
the great Pauline phrase." He looks from God's truth to the
other parts of God's truth not enshrined in Scripture, and
yearns to integrate all into " that spiritual truth revealed in

the Bible and incarnate in Christ." [29]

Dr. Gaebelein subscribes to the view that God's Word is to be found in nature as well as in Scripture. He also has a high regard for reason, which, enlightened by the Holy Spirit, can apprehend God's truth. The most effective means of integration of truth in its various forms is through the person of the Christian teacher. A teacher who is saturated with the Spirit of Christ will be able to communicate integrated truth to his pupils, whether the subject he teaches is mathematics, literature, or history. Indeed, he would like to see in every Christian school (this would of necessity exclude the public schools because of the legal situation) a corps of teachers so thoroughly committed to God's truth that a completely separate department of the Bible would be unnecessary. All teachers would be competent to offer instruction in the Bible, and, indeed, would do so as a part of their regular duties.[30]

Reviewing *The Pattern of God's Truth*, Howard Grimes raises questions at two points regarding Gaebelein's argument. He feels that Gaebelein takes a dangerous stand in equating the written word of the Bible with God's truth, for this " is to ignore biblical scholarship of the nineteenth century as well as current biblical theology." Grimes feels, too, that Gaebelein's rationalistic structure for the supporting of Biblical truth misses the meaning of faith as contrasted to reason. " He almost says — but not quite — that the biblical faith gives a context and a basis for the work of human reason, but in the final analysis he seems to be shoring up the biblical faith by a rational structure. He is willing to admit that the world is more than six thousand years old, but not that biblical science is wrong." [31]

Elsewhere Dr. Gaebelein has written on " The Task of Christian Education " as producing seven distinctive challenges to evangelicals: (1) to study and formulate an adequate philosophy of education for "their kind of education"; (2) an increased awareness of higher intellectual standards as an obligatory accompaniment for Christian education; (3) "a new consciousness of the relation of Christianity to culture"; (4) "a penetration of the isolationism of evangelical education through the recognition of values in the educational philosophy and practice of Christian groups not commonly associated with evangelicalism"; (5) more attention paid to elementary and secondary education; (6) not shirking responsibility for public education in the deep concern for Christian day schools; (7) "a growing drive on the part of evangelicalism toward a more articulate and competent scholarship, especially on the graduate and seminary levels." [32]

Dr. Gaebelein's writings display a high intellectual interest and a level of thought obviously designed to interest liberals, neoorthodox, syncretists, as well as the various types of fundamentalists. It will be seen that his rationalistic concern makes him very akin to the liberalist continuum, whose adherents, however, would reject his intellectual presuppositions as radically as Gaebelein would reject theirs. Thomists also, as we shall see in the next chapter, would find themselves in agreeable company with Gaebelein because of his making so large a place for reason alongside (or in relation to) faith, whereas existentialist thinkers would question whether he pays adequate attention to the ambivalence of the human situation and motivation. The home is viewed culturally as having a burden of education to bear rather than in terms of its being an "order of society." Does Gaebelein differentiate sufficiently between the vocation to be a Christian and the vocation to be a teacher? Does he firmly enough differentiate between preaching and teaching and the relationship between the two? Does he explain how propositional truth can be expected to carry the dynamic Christian gospel? Is there a tendency to think of the Sunday church school as having a sort of divine prerogative almost apart from the nurturing church community as a whole? To staff the ideal Christian school, where would one find adequate numbers of competent scholars to do effective teaching of geography, mathematics, history, etc.? Are there to be " tests " of orthodoxy for students and teachers in order to maintain the purity of the Christian school?

In one sense the argument for integration which Frank Gaebelein adduces is a fresh form of the ancient debate (*vide* Tertullian) about the relation between Athens and Jerusalem. Unlike Tertullian, who strongly opposed too much commerce (if any) between the sacred and the secular disciplines, Gaebelein seems to this extent to be very much a product of the opponents of Tertullian, who saw all truth as one. There is the final question, however, as to whether the concept of " integration " itself is an appropriate Biblical one, or does it stem instead from the Greeks? Does that somewhat alter the debate? Does Gaebelein then become, in that sense, a humanistic rationalist, as over against the neoorothodox, who have insisted that the Bible should not be pressed into any philosophic mold other than its own ethos and milieu?

Strict Calvinistic fundamentalism is represented in a volume entitled *Fundamentals in Christian Education: Theory and Practice,* edited by Cornelius Jaarsma, professor of education in Calvin College. Those desiring to see another facet of the fundamentalist–neo-evangelical approach to education might well consult Jaarsma's book

to see how a tradition that has always had a strong intellec-
tualistic emphasis stands within the fundamentalistic-Bib-
licistic stance. The book contains chapters by a number of
Dutch theologians as well as Americans involved in the
Christian day schools of the Christian Reformed Church
and the colleges and seminaries of the fundamentalist-
Calvinistic persuasions.[33]

7

Ferment Within Roman Catholicism

Most Protestants have entertained a rather stereotyped notion of Roman Catholic education, based indeed on an image that often has been projected in the past by American Roman Catholic parochial schools. Traditionally, these have been thought to be concerned with passing on the Catholic faith in a regimented fashion, "parochial" in the pejorative sense of the word and methodologically old-fashioned.

The fact of the matter is that this stereotype probably never was totally legitimate, overlooking as it did some of the truly experimental efforts at improving parish education in which the Roman Church has been engaged in some places for years. It is noteworthy that for many years Roman Catholic teaching nuns and brothers and clergy have been attending teachers colleges in significant centers like New York, Philadelphia, and Chicago, borrowing ideas from public school education which could be adapted to parish school situations. As long ago as 1929, Mary Helen Mayer, in the introductory essay to her translation of Thomas Aquinas' *De Magistro*, portrayed Thomas Aquinas as methodologically almost Deweyan in his thrust.[1] The old-fashioned stereotype of the parochial school, even as held by Roman Catholics themselves who were brought up under the severe disciplinary methods of yesteryear, is about as irrelevant to present-day facts as the one-room schoolhouse in rural America, which nurtured the young people of the 1870's and 1880's. Both would be hard to find in typical contemporary communities.

THE CATECHETICAL REVOLUTION

The real revolution in catechetics (the term used by most Roman Catholic writers to refer to the whole process of religious nurture) began in Europe after World War I. Pierre Ranwez has referred to that period as " a crisis in religious instruction." The catechetical classes, it was beginning to be realized, were deductive and abstract, whereas " only the concrete . . . interests the child "; they dealt with expository material that involved the child but little; they were ill-adapted to the wide variety of personalities among the learners. Father Ranwez quotes from a pastoral letter of 1922 written by the Bishop of Dijon, Monsignor Landrieux, which " became a kind of manifesto of the catechetical revival ": " Instead of going in directly by the open doors of the child's imagination and sense perception, we waste our time knocking on the still bolted doors of his understanding and his judgment." The bishop urged teachers to expose their pupils to the gospel itself, offering personal contact with Jesus Christ, before attempting to teach their children the details of Christian theology.[2]

From that time on, various individual writers began to experiment with new kinds of lesson materials, and adventurous teachers became bold to try new methods of teaching. Meanwhile, the liturgical movement, led by priests such as Abbé Michonneau of Paris, was leading to a rethinking of the life of parishes in every aspect, including catechesis. A close correlation between the life of the worshiping congregation and what was taught in the catechetical classes was encouraged. Instruction that was related to the Biblical and other liturgical materials was increasingly a part of the church life, and persons of all ages were involved in " the rites with their verbal and gestural forms, colors, poetry, and music " — all of which " proclaim the message and give some advance idea of what needs to be rendered clearer," as Father Ranwez puts it.[3]

In 1960 these researches converged into a full-scale International Study Week on Missionary Catechetics, convened at Eichstätt. At that congress papers on a wide range of subjects related to contemporary catechetics were presented by persons active in church teaching throughout the Roman Catholic Church. These papers have been published in *Teaching All Nations: A Symposium on Modern Catechetics*.[4] They treat such subjects as kerygmatic renewal, methodological changes, books for teaching, the relation of teaching to worship, the concept of the revived catechumenate, and training and helping catechists.

Several selections from the " General Conclusions " of the Eichstätt congress are so important as to need reproduction here in order that we may see the far-reaching scope of the mid-twentieth century Roman Catholic catechetical renewal.

Thus, on liturgy:

There is latent in the liturgy a colossal wealth of meaning and a tremendous instructive power. These lie in its prayers, songs, and readings; in the actions of the priest and people, the frequency of its celebration and the assembly for it of all the faithful. Therefore, the liturgy should be celebrated in a manner which will bring out to the full its catechetical content, and which will enable people to take an active part in it devoutly and intelligently. Hence, in order that the liturgy may produce its due catechetical effect, it should display its intrinsic excellences by means of its intelligibility, beauty, and clarity. Only thus can its full catechetical value be exploited.[5]

Concerning the Bible:

The Bible must be given a very prominent place in catechetical teaching because it is the inspired Word of God, and the most important of all the church's didactic books. It sets forth the divine actions whereby God has revealed himself; its method of presentation is so vivid and lively that it is suited to man's capacities, and it is explicitly ordered towards man's salvation. Hence catechetics must be solidly built up on a biblical foundation; every age group should be taught biblical texts and made familiar with events in biblical history.[6]

Again, regarding catechists (that is, lay teachers), it is written:

All catechists should have at least one year of solid training. This must impart to them above all a complete grasp of the fundamentals of Christian doctrine concerning man's salvation, together with an adequate competence in catechetical methods. At the same time great stress must be laid on the spiritual training and character formation given to catechists as well as on their social behavior, so that they may become not only good teachers, but also " witnesses to Christ." In their religious training, the Bible and the liturgy must be given the prominent place due them in the catechetical apostolate later on.[7]

It is instructive to ponder statements like the above in the light of recent curricular developments and theoretical reconstructions of educational principles within the Protestant traditions. The similarities, or at least correspondences, are quite marked in many instances. This is again apparent when one reads the statement of "Basic Principles of Modern Catechetics" as adopted at Eichstätt. There are references to the proclamation of God's message of salvation to all men, the Christ-centeredness of catechetics, the call to respond to God "by an inner change of heart manifested in a life of faith and hope and of loving obedience to his commands," the need to relate teaching "to the life and thought of people," the function of catechesis in introducing "the catechumen into a living community," helping him "to strike root in it." [8]

That this has indeed been a revolutionary movement is evidenced by a new spirit of openness and dialogue which has characterized Roman Catholic teachers and clergy in recent years. At one of the Catholic colleges for women in the Chicago area, for example, an effort is being made to integrate into the library and teaching program representative Protestant curriculum materials as well as general works on Protestant religious education. The spirit animating the recent developments in catechetics is similar to that emerging from the Vatican Council — *aggiornamento* — bringing the church into a lively contact with the real world of today where people actually dwell.

THE FORMATION OF THE TRUE CHRISTIAN:
Rappresentanti in terra

Any discussion of the nature of the Roman Catholic educational thought must take into consideration the encyclical letter of Pope Pius XI (1929) entitled *Rappresentanti in terra* (sometimes referred to also as *Divini illius ma-*

gistri), popularly known in English as " The Christian Education of Youth." It must be remembered that this document was produced prior to some of the more revolutionary developments of the Second Vatican Council.

In this document, the pope first speaks of the importance of education and of the importance of seeing from the beginning how the whole work of education is intimately and necessarily connected with its proper last end: " preparing man for what he must be and for what he must do here below, in order to attain the sublime end for which he was created." [9] He then takes up, in order, " who has the mission to educate; who are the subjects to be educated; what are the necessary accompanying circumstances; what is the end and object proper to Christian education according to God's established order in the economy of his divine providence." [10]

The orders of society are described as of two types: those belonging to the " natural order " — family and civil state; that belonging to the " supernatural order " — the church. The preeminent right to educate belongs first to the church by virtue of its supernatural order " conferred exclusively upon her by God himself " — attested to by the magisterial commission conferred by Christ upon his church and by the church's " supernatural motherhood, in virtue of which the church, spotless spouse of Christ, generates, nurtures, and educates souls in the divine life of grace with her sacraments and her doctrine." [11]

It follows, then, that " it is the inalienable right as well as the indispensable duty of the church to watch over the entire education of her children, that is the faithful, in all institutions, public or private, not merely in regard to the religious instruction there given, but in regard to every other branch of learning and every regulation insofar as

religion and morality are concerned." [12] Nor is the church
to confine her educational activity only to the faithful, for
it is called upon to teach all whom it can reach, " seeing
that all men are called to enter the kingdom of God and
reach eternal salvation." [13] The relation of the family to
this educational responsibility, which is the prime right
of the church, is one of cooperation with the church: " the
church placing at the disposal of families her office of mis-
tress and educator, and the families eager to profit by the
offer, and entrusting their children to the church in hundreds and thousands." [14]

The roles of the church and family are clear. What, then,
is the role of the state? That is equally clear, according to
the encyclical. Since the state has been entrusted with the
duty of protecting the temporal welfare of its citizenry,
it must protect by law the rights of the church and family
with regard to their prior claim on the privilege of edu-
cating and " promote in various way the education and
instruction of youth," including the provision of civic education for its citizens. Between the church and state there
should exist a fine harmony based on a mutual recognition
of the proper spheres of influence of each. [15]

In the concluding sections of the encyclical is the much-
quoted " purpose " of Christian education: " The proper
and immediate end of Christian education is to cooperate
with divine grace in forming the true and perfect Christian, that is, to form Christ himself in those regenerated
by Baptism. . . . For precisely this reason, Christian education takes in the whole aggregate of human life, physical
and spiritual, intellectual and moral, individual, domestic,
and social, not with a view of reducing it in any way, but
in order to elevate, regulate, and perfect it, in accordance
with the example and teaching of Christ." [16]

Church education, therefore, does not seek to prepare people for a life isolated from the common life of man, but a life that will go into the world to lift it to the level of Christ — the "Christ transforming culture" motif as well as the "Christ above culture" one, to use Richard Niebuhr's famous categories.[17] "The true Christian does not renounce the activities of this life; he does not stunt his natural faculties, but he develops and perfects them by coordinating them with the supernatural. He thus ennobles what is merely natural in life and secures for it new strength in the material and temporal order, no less than in the spiritual and eternal."[18]

Although there is considerable discussion within Roman Catholic theological circles as to the exact status of papal encyclicals with regard to normative doctrine (the pope speaks ex cathedra only in matters of dogma — faith and morals — which then become binding on all believers), probably most Roman Catholic theologians would hesitate long before minimizing the importance of these documents. The late Gustave Weigel has pointed out that one must read the encyclicals with a recognition that "there is always an historical factor in papal teaching. The pope speaks for a definite moment of time, though he communicates a trans-historical message." However, as Father Weigel says, "papal doctrine is undoubtedly the most authentic expression of Catholic beliefs and positions."[19]

When one deals with contemporary catechetical theorists, therefore, one must always see their work as being done with the papal teachings clearly in mind, though they are always quite free, within the principles of accepted theology, to venture forth bravely in new directions. This is not always done without struggle, of course; yet it is something to be pondered by Protestants, who always have been proud of their freedom of action, that in the present situation the Roman Catholic Church can embrace new practices, and even interpretations, within a continuing " system."

TEACHING THE MYSTERY OF CHRIST:

Johannes Hofinger

The European catechetical movement within the Roman Church has elicited several formidable leaders. One center of research and rethinking has been the Institute for Religious Education, Brussels, whose quarterly journal, *Lumen Vitae*, is available in an English edition. A pivotal figure in the liturgical movement and its associated catechetical aspects has been Josef Andreas Jungmann, S.J., rector of the Canisianum in Innsbruck. Father Jungmann has held the chair of catechetics in Innsbruck, though he is equally distinguished for his work in liturgics. The theologian Karl Rahner, S.J., has also contributed much by way of seminal ideas.

In this country another Jesuit, Johannes Hofinger, now at the University of Notre Dame, has done much through his writing and the leadership of conferences to further the new concern with catechetics. One of the most stimulating books in this area is his *The Art of Teaching Christian Doctrine: The Good News and Its Proclamation*, published in 1957 while he was associated with the Institute for Mission Apologetics in Manila. It is written in four parts: the task, the structure of the message, the essential content of the message, and the training of catechists.

Father Hofinger takes a retrospective view of the older catechetical methods and the " lengthy, difficult and pictureless catechisms, . . . splendid models, no doubt, of precise formulation of the church's doctrine, but equally splendid models of a completely unpsychological presentation of that doctrine." [20] He outlines the characteristic emphases within the catechetical renewal: the need to adapt religious instruction to the psychology of the child; the need to develop religious dispositions and convictions in children as well as to communicate religious knowledge to them. He argues for a " radically Christian " view of the catechetical apostolate, which will not be concerned only, or even primarily, with methodology, but will ask the more important questions: "What are we to teach; what is the central core of the message we are to proclaim; what are the essential doctrines we should stress; from what viewpoint should we present this message so that it becomes truly the ' Gospel ' of our Lord; what would be the best arrangement of the catechetical material for the purpose of leading our pupils to understand it in a rightly religious way and to make use of it in their daily lives? " [21]

He postulates as the " central theme " what he refers to as " the mystery of Christ." This central mystery, which it is the task of the church to proclaim, is really the gospel: " the message of the unfathomable riches that are given to us in Christ, . . . the good tidings of our salvation in Christ; he has . . . *visited* us, given himself for us, and taken us home to himself, not only each of us individually, but all of us together in the wonderful unity which we form through our living connection with Christ in his mystical Body." The teaching task is to provide not only knowledge of this mystery of Christ but participation in it. That is, " we are to help the maturing Christian gradually to become aware of the magnificence of his vocation and of the greatness of his task in life as a Christian." [22]

The means into the mystery are the Bible, the liturgy, doctrine, and Christian living, to each of which Father Hofinger devotes a chapter. Of Bible teaching he warns: " Bible history, even in the very first grades, is far more than a series of beautiful stories about Christ, far more than the life of Christ told in a childlike way. It is the introduction into the Christian religion by way of Bible history." [23] He approaches the category of historical re-presentation when he says that " religious instruction is, from the very beginning, not so much history as ' mystagogy '! With this particular ' history,' it is always a question of the present. . . . What the loving Father has done for us from the beginning of creation up to today is the basis of our present life and actions." [24]

The liturgy is conceived as presenting the mystery of Christ. The stories and other materials should be correlated with the liturgical year in such a way that the children are living out what they learn. He calls to mind Father Jungmann's principle: " Not much liturgics, but much liturgy," for these could be a subtle temptation to study a great deal about the church seasons, altar appointments, colors, etc., without becoming immersed in the realities of which these other matters are mere symbols.[25]

However, systematic instruction in doctrine should also have a place in catechetics. This should not be forced before the person is ready to undertake such a systematization of material. Still, even this didactic necessity must not be done in isolation. " The systematic religious instruction to be given in the upper grades has . . . to fulfill an important intellectual task. It is to contribute to a fuller intellectual penetration of Christian doctrine. But we must not conclude from this fact that this instruction should be any the less concerned with Christian life than is the instruction given in the primary grades." He warns that " systematic " does not mean " theoretic and remote from life." " Systematic instruction is justified to the degree to which it helps the student to perceive Christian doctrine as a compact mystery and its value in his life." [26]

Father Hofinger has an interesting discussion of the differences between the traditional scholastic theological approach and the newer approach via the kerygmatic theology. They have different goals. " Scholastic theology aims primarily at an intellectual elaboration of Christian doctrine. It calls, therefore, for formulations that are as precise as possible, for solid argumentation with a manifest preference for syllogistic form and deduction." Kerygmatic theology, on the other hand, " aims at the religious appreciation and the missionary proclamation of the revealed truth," striving " to understand Christian doctrine in relation to Christian living, to bring out its religious values."

Their objects, also, are different. Scholastic theology is concerned with the whole truth (as the theologians often composed *summae theologicae* — summaries of the whole body of theological knowledge). Kerygmatic theology is more modest. It seeks to emphasize " those aspects of revealed truth which are in a special way meant to be lived and proclaimed." Likewise, the values are different. Orthodoxy, a clear distinction between truth and error, is the chief value for the former. The kerygmatic approach is more interested in the sense of the matter, the manifestations of doctrine in " the ability to pray, to meditate, to appreciate, to live Christian doctrine." [27] Setting forth these differences is not intended by Father Hofinger to say that one is rigidly wrong and the other perfectly right. He is concerned simply to highlight the fact that the kerygmatic approach does introduce a new and different dimension into the teaching of the Christian faith, which was not realized until the stranglehold of older, more "orthodox" methodology had been broken.

EXISTENTIALIST THOMISM: *Jacques Maritain*

Jacques Maritain is generally recognized as being one of the few "universal" men of our times. He looks at life *sub specie aeternitatis* and at the same time with an awareness of immediate detail; he knows and appreciates art, literature, philosophy, and science, and possesses insights into the meaning of culture that are characterized by penetration and imaginative feeling. Primarily a philosopher, he also is a competent theologian, as well as a man of affairs and a student of general culture. He represented the Vatican as ambassador to France at one time, and lived for many years in Princeton, where he held a chair in the philosophy department at the university. One speaks of him in the same breath with contemporaries such as the late Albert Einstein, or Albert Schweitzer, Martin Buber, and Karl Barth — persons of gargantuan intellectual attainment and universal sympathies. With Étienne Gilson, Maritain is generally regarded as one of the two foremost Thomistic philosophers of this century. Although he is now very old and in almost complete retirement, he continues to publish writings which command wide attention.

He does not regard himself as a scholastic Thomist in the narrower sense in which scholasticism was defined above. That is, he is not out to amass innumerable factual statements, or to prove many points with syllogistic perfection of argument. He prefers, in fact, to call himself an existentialist. He certainly would not qualify as an existentialist in the usual categories of secular existentialist thought, but he has an affinity for the concrete experience, the inner decision, the freedom of the person in the sight of God — all of which are typical existentialist modes of thinking, feeling, and acting. If " Christian existentialist Thomism " is a possible category, then Jacques Maritain should be classified that way, even though some Thomists would scarcely recognize his as a pure form of their brand of thought, and existentialists might regard him as a very traditionalist, even " scholastic " kind of bedfellow.

Maritain has not written systematically on education in any long treatise, although *Education at the Crossroads*, which is our immediate interest, is his near approach to a " systematic pedagogy." We are indebted to Donald and Idella Gallagher, of Boston College, for their collection of miscellaneous educational essays by Maritain which have been published under the title *The Education of Man*.[28]

Education at the Crossroads consists of the Terry Lectures for 1943 at Yale University. He says that " The Education of Man " (the title the Gallaghers have chosen to give their anthology) would have been his preferred choice for a title, save that he was afraid it might have been misunderstood in terms of being provocative: " for many of our contemporaries know primitive man, or Western man, or the man of the Renaissance, or the man of the industrial era, or the criminal man, or the bourgeois man, or the working man, but they wonder what is meant when we speak of man." [29] (For other reasons, many of us can be glad he did not choose a title already associated with a great pedagogical work by Friedrich Froebel). It is about man, indeed, that he proceeds to write in the entire work.

Maritain's concept of man is that man is not merely " an

animal of nature, like a skylark or a bear. He is also an animal of culture, whose race can subsist only within the
development of society and civilization, he is an *historical*
animal: hence the multiplicity of cultural or ethico-histor-
ical patterns into which man is diversified; hence, too, the
essential importance of education." [30] To become truly
man, to be genuinely educated, man must undergo discipline and participate in tradition — for his humanity is
bound up with the culture to which he is heir.

He proceeds to demolish one by one seven " misconcep-
tions " which he thinks have tended to warp a proper view
of education in the twentieth century. These are as follows: (1) a tendency to put so much stress on the means
— which in general are better than education has ever before had available — that the ends are disregarded; (2) the
nature of the end of man is itself blurred and confused
because we have settled for " the purely scientific idea
of man " which is " a phenomenalized idea without reference to ultimate reality," whereas the philosophical-re-
ligious idea of man deals with " the essential and intrinsic,
though not visible or tangible characters " of man; (3) the
pragmatic philosophy has ended up with " a psychological
worship of the subject," that is, an emphasis on the pupil's
growth as being more interesting and important than " the
object to be taught and the primacy of the object ";
(4) what he calls " sociologism " refers to the tendency to
adapt men to " the conditions and interactions of social
life " rather than first " making a man "; (5) the modern
form of " intellectualism " tends to give up universal values
and it views education in terms of scientific or technical
specialization; (6) by " voluntarism " he means subordi-
nating the training of the mind to the training of the will
as a goal of education, and he rejects this on the ground

that the will cannot be effectively taught as a separate goal; (7) not everything can be learned, as modern pedagogy has tended to think — for example, prudence and wisdom, which result only from spiritual experience.[31]

He attempts to formulate some "fundamental norms of education," which he calls "rules," though not in a legalistic sense. These are: (1) "foster those fundamental dispositions which enable the principal agent to grow in the life of the mind" (that is, the teacher must seek to liberate the student's mind); (2) "center attention on the inner depths of personality and its preconscious spiritual dynamism" (that is, strive always to internalize learning); (3) education should unify man's life, not spread it out over too wide a terrain (this being very difficult the more knowledge is produced in the world); (4) teaching should "liberate intelligence instead of burdening it" (reason should come to have mastery over what has been learned.) [32]

After outlining some curricular suggestions regarding the contemporary understanding of the liberal arts in relation to total humane learning and the Christian synthesis, Maritain concludes with a chapter entitled "The Trials of Present-Day Education." He feels that liberal education is not only grounded in the true ends of man — and therefore the true ends of man's education — but also that the modern world poses some special difficulties which only this kind of education can meet. He argues for what he calls "an integral education for an integral humanism." He fears that the individualistic society of the past, now doomed, will be replaced by new totalitarianisms unless it is based on "a personalistic and communal civilization, grounded on human rights and satisfying the social aspirations and needs of man."

Part of this must be the bringing to an end of " the cleavage between religious inspiration and secular activity in man." He believes that the relations between state and school must be properly understood, and argues for the freedom of private groups of parents and others to offer education as they desire. (This is reminiscent of *Rappresentanti in terra*). The present crisis in morality, he thinks, can only be met by the training of children " in proper conduct, law observance, and politeness," and that these must be based on true " internal formation," though he does not spell out how this is to be accomplished, save to suggest that brotherly love needs to be inculcated in families.[38] Always, he is concerned to address the principle to the concrete situation. This is Maritain's " existentialist Thomism."

The educational pattern of the Roman Catholic Church is a broad and inclusive one, ranging from parish schools to the great Jesuit universities, from lay catechists in jungle country to the researchers of *Lumen Vitae*. At times it may have been a slumbering giant. Its muscles are today toned up for massive work. It has had no left-wing movement to reckon with, such as H. Shelton Smith saw liberalist religious education to be, but it has had its own right-wing scholastic conservatism. Neither was a mere Don Quixotean windmill against which to have to tilt. Rome has been having its catechetical renaissance comparable to the reconstruction that has taken place within Protestant educational theory. Both are informed by similar currents springing from the same streams of vital Christian faith: the apostolic and Biblical faith, however differently " Protestants and Catholics " may interpret it to themselves.

8

Accent Upon the Church

In addition to the recognizable " groups " or " types " of writers dealing with religious education theory whom we have discussed thus far, there are some others who scarcely can be said to constitute a " group," but nevertheless deal with one central subject which in a sense make one think of them corporately. The subject is the church. There, however, it must be admitted, the similarity ends, for the ways in which they conceive of the church are quite different from one another. But this does not mean to suggest that they have nothing in common with regard to the doctrine of the church — merely, that they have chosen to take their stance within particular traditions or with special intentions in mind.

By referring to these writers who put an especial accent upon the church, furthermore, one does not mean thereby to imply that the others whom we have discussed have any less a church-oriented type of nurture. After all, several of them have used " church " in their book titles, and the doctrine of the *ekklēsia* can be found highlighted on many of their pages. The writers whom we shall discuss now merely happen to slant their perspective with more or less deliberate attention to ecclesiological concerns.

THE REDEMPTIVE COMMUNITY: *Howard Grimes*

In two books, Howard Grimes, professor of Christian education in Perkins School of Theology, Southern Methodist University, has essayed a study of the nature of the church. The first, *The Church Redemptive*, appeared in 1958; the second, *The Rebirth of the Laity*, came out in 1962. The ecclesiological foundations for nurture thus appear to be a major concern of Professor Grimes.

In *The Church Redemptive* he states that three " central convictions" underlay his writing of the book. He thinks that Protestantism has been failing in an understanding of the meaning of church *as* church, tending to interpret church principally in terms of its institutional or cultural nature. He thinks, further, that the church will not be able to act as such until it *does* understand its own destiny and purpose. Third, he chooses to put primary emphasis on the view that the church is the *laos,* the people of God.

In Part I he sets forth some understandings regarding the nature of the church, freely admitting divergences and disagreements among Christians on this matter. Using F. W. Dillistone's categories of " the imperial " and " the contractual " views of the church, and finding both unacceptable in terms of what the church really is, he goes on to the categories of the church as an organism and the church as a covenant community. He thinks that these two views are corrective of each other and need to be held in tension.

Grimes states his view thus: " The Church is a gift of God, bestowed upon us because of his grace; yet each of us must appropriate this gift through faith. It is a unity into which we are accepted through no merit of our own;

it is a community where those who are accepted pledge their faith each to the other because of their common faith in the God and Father of our Lord Jesus Christ. . . . Unless the life of the Church is carried on with a keen sense of its divine nature, that life may easily become secularized and the Church may become only a society for human betterment. . . . It is the Body of Christ; yet we are individually responsible." [1]

He then proceeds to interpret the church in terms of imagery appropriate to the " people of God " motif, interpreting what this means in terms of the priesthood of believers and the ministry of the laity. He writes of the *koinōnia* in its New Testament sense, pointing out the misinterpretations that church people often have made of the idea of " fellowship." " This failure of the Church to be a redemptive fellowship poses for us the problem of a starting point for its transformation and renewal. If God must work through us, where do we begin? " Here, in company with another group of theorists, Grimes takes his stand in terms of relationship theology. " The beginning of such a transformation is in relationships." [2]

Next, Howard Grimes goes on to a consideration of the work of the church as the redemptive community. First he discusses the church as a worshiping community. He contrasts the subjectively and objectively oriented types of worship to be found in Protestantism today. One type of worship is interested primarily in " creating a mood, producing a good feeling, inspiring action," whereas Christian worship for the people of God must always be a corporate offering, " a re-enactment of the drama of redemption not by a group of players (minister, choir, organist) for the congregation to watch what is done, but rather by a congregation . . . every person being an actor in the drama." [3]

He also stresses the recovery of the sacramental sense, focused especially in a fuller understanding of Baptism and the Lord's Supper.

In a chapter entitled " Nurturing Life Within the Christian Community," Grimes deals especially with education as a function of the *koinōnia*. He makes several assertions: (1) Christian teaching must be church-centered; (2) learning involves all the influences making a person what he becomes; (3) nurture pertains to all ages, birth to death; (4) the family as a unit must be reckoned with in Christian nurture; (5) the curriculum's heart of content will be " creative encounter — between man and man and between man and God," this taking place in community. He offers a definition of the purpose of Christian education: " to seek to lead persons into a living encounter with the God and Father of our Lord Jesus Christ, and to illuminate and enlighten the meaning of this encounter for all of life." [4]

Grimes expresses concern for the quality of group life within the fellowship, the training of leaders, the evangelistic outreach of the community (interpreted in terms of " mission "), and administrative methods conceived as related to " purposes not exterior to the life of the agency (such as the Church), but those inherent within the nature of the agency itself (or so far as the Church is concerned in the Christian Gospel)." [5]

In *The Rebirth of the Laity*, Dr. Grimes seeks to penetrate farther into the meaning of the corporate life of the *laos* by examining in detail the role of the laity in the life of the contemporary Christian church. He states the Biblical background of the theology of the laity and describes some aspects of the role of the laity in the historical development of the church. He delineates some twentieth-century "problems and prospects": the tendency of American churches to serve their communities primarily as social organizations; the promotional mentality which has gripped some aspects of church life, especially in denominational boards and agencies; the rise of multiple staff ministries, accompanied by a tendency for the clergy to be directors of "the army of lay workers"; the rise of incipient anticlericalism that takes the form of lay opposition to clergy involvement in social issues.

Grimes interprets the work of the laity in its "gathered" state — that is, assembled for worship and learning and in its "dispersed" state — the laity's being the church in the world, "witnessing to their faith in those realms of culture outside the corporate life of the church." (David R. Hunter speaks later, in *Christian Education as Engagement*, of the church gathered and scattered — equivalent concepts.) In the "dispersed" state Christians work out their Christian vocation, exercise Christian charity (service), and make a Christian witness. He uses the term "lay apostolate," which, as we have seen, is much used in the Roman Catholic Church. Final chapters deal with emerging patterns of renewal (European and American) and means toward renewal (group life, study areas). It is obvious that in the mission of the church there will be, according to Howard Grimes, expansive opportunities for witness and service in every aspect of the church's life, including its teaching ministry.[6] "We dare not be so presumptuous," Professor Grimes writes, "as to say that a real revival in the church is occurring, but there are enough evidences of it that we can at least hope that such is the case."[7]

THE SACRAMENTAL PRINCIPLE: *Dora P. Chaplin*

In 1948, Dora P. Chaplin, who then was involved in Christian education work in an Episcopal parish in Greater Boston, produced the work entitled *Children and Religion*. Her publishers brought out a revised, second edition in 1961. In her Introduction to the second edition, Mrs. Chaplin refers to the experience of rereading one's own book written sometime ago as being in ways "like the perusal of work done by another person." She did not alter her essential arguments, in spite of the passage of time, for these seemed to her still valid: "A whole new educational vocabulary has risen up, and now, like all the others, it shows signs of being dethroned. But Christianity is Christ, and Christ does not change. In the midst of all the changing circumstances of new civilizations, the church on earth as the gospel-bearing people of God, remains at worship and at work. The task is not different, the good news of man's creation by God and redemption in Christ is still ultimate truth." [8]

Mrs. Chaplin does not identify the "whole new educational vocabulary" which she thinks is now probably being dethroned. Does she mean a vocabulary that grew up between 1948 and 1961? Or does she refer to the period of the Coe ascendancy as far as the earlier period is concerned? Actually, by referring to the abidingness of Christ and the church, she is saying in this Introduction something that has been implicit in her own thinking for a long time but became explicit only in her later work, *The Privilege of Teaching*, published in 1962.

There she states her central principle very clearly. "Our constant aim," she writes, "in the education of a Christian is to lead him, through his sacramental life in the church's

worship and work, to discover almighty God in Christ
Jesus and to be transformed to God's will and purpose, in
this world and the next." What does Mrs. Chaplin mean by
" the sacramental life "? [9] She elaborates on this phrase
elsewhere, as follows: " The sacramental life is the life in
which the individual *accepts* the offering of God's own
self through God-chosen means. Through the simple acts
of washing and feeding, made holy in Baptism and in the
Eucharist, a Christian discovers his unique relationship
with God as a member of the Body of Christ. A life opened
up to God and transformed by him is called a sacramental
life." [10]

She states also that " the Christian teacher's work, as the
work of one of the people of God, cannot be separated
from the purpose of the whole church, which is the people
of God." And that purpose of the church is to worship God,
to sanctify the faithful, reach out to the unchurched, and
prepare the world for the Kingdom of God. The purpose
of the church is thus defined in terms of the work of the
church, which, ontologically speaking, is the work of Christ
himself. " ' The Church ' indicates the state of being ' in
Christ,' not merely ' related to him '; it signifies actually *being incorporated into Christ,* beginning with Baptism." [11]

It is this concern with what we have called " the sacramental principle " that would seem to be Dora Chaplin's
major emphasis. In it we see the reflection of an expression
that is close to the heart of the Anglo-Catholic tradition.
The teacher's personal devotional life is deemed of pivotal
importance, for it is out of his own practice of " the life
of prayer " that he will be able to reach his pupils deeply.
Belief in God comes first, for " the kind of prayers we pray
depend upon the kind of God we believe in." [12] " We can
only become what we are, or rather, what God intended

us to be, through his grace. . . . It matters supremely whether or not we say our prayers. . . . The teacher's life and work (are to be seen) as instruments of God." [13] These are all ways of speaking that grow out of ascetic or mystical theology, as these are referred to in the particular Anglican tradition out of which Mrs. Chaplin speaks. She was born in England. She served for several years as associate secretary in the department of leadership training of the National Council of the Protestant Episcopal Church. She has taught for some years as the only woman faculty member in the General Theological Seminary, a Protestant Episcopal Church institution in New York City, where she is now professor of Christian education. Kenyon College awarded her an honorary degree of doctor of sacred theology.

CHURCH EDUCATION: Wesner Fallaw

Wesner Fallaw, of Andover Newton Theological School, where he is Howard Professor of Religious Education, served as a pastor in Congregational churches before entering teaching. While on the staff of the Congregational church in Winnetka, Illinois, he was engaged in a number of experimental program efforts related to getting parents involved in the Christian education enterprise. These experiences led to his writing of *The Modern Parent and the Teaching Church*,[14] which for many years was the only book of weighty influence in the fairly new field of parent education, and consequently has appeared on practically every religious education bibliography since it was issued in 1946.

In *Church Education for Tomorrow* (1960), Dr. Fallaw proposed a thesis that was shattering to many in the church who had inherited a century and a half of confidence in the essentiality and improvability of the Sunday school. He was now saying that this time-honored (and time-bound) institution of the Sunday school should be exposed to radical rethinking. He personally was convinced that it had seen its best days and was now moribund, if far from actually deceased as yet. In place of Sunday school education, he desires to introduce what he chooses to call " church education." That is how he enters the picture with regard to this present chapter's classification of " church " types of Christian education.

If the Sunday school, as a division of the church, sufficed in the past to bring up children in the life of faith, now the church in its wholeness — with fully qualified professionals doing the teaching — needs to essay the nurture task. Not the traditional Sunday school but church education is requisite for our times, for the day of Biblical knowledge is far spent and the night of Christian faith and hope and love lowers on atomic clouds. Aside from shallow moralisms, too often typical of casual or even pious Sunday school efforts, the profound meaning of Christian belief ought to be articulated and learned. The moment a pastor and his people grasp the importance of nurture and perceive the wisdom of conserving the pastor's time and talent for primary things, that moment a new departure will be taken in Christian teaching and pastoral care. Then will the church as fellowship control the church as institution, and the chosen leader can drop the role of promoter in chief and resume his calling as true shepherd.[15]

By " church education," Dr. Fallaw means " a teaching-learning enterprise, grounded in theology and Scripture, whose goal is that of enabling persons to learn of God through Christ as experienced in Christian community, the church." [16] It is through the life, worship, action, and thought of a parish church that individuals and the whole congregation receive nurture. Only the true household of God will be able to train a novice in grace and knowledge of God. " Created for community, our complete growth is only afforded by means of Christian community." [17]

That Wesner Fallaw means by " church education " a theologically responsible nurture which takes the Biblical milieu with earnest seriousness is demonstrated in the way he contrasts " religious education " and " church education." This might be put into chart form, something as follows:

Religious Education	Church Education
Truth can be " found."	The Bible provides the norm of faith and life.
Works more or less independently of the church.	Is the church expressing itself in the nurture process.
Character development.	Probes depths of personality, striving for reconciliation.
Good life in this world.	Life in time and eternity.

He envisions church education as fulfilling religious education. " The two are not wholly opposite, either in conception or in program " (this in spite of the rather stark contrasts shown above). " It now becomes the task of the church to minister according to the fullness and richness of its being, as a worshiping community teaching by influence and by systematic pastoral instruction." [18]

In the execution of church education, Fallaw sees the pastor as the chief teacher. He will teach the older children and have lay assistants (if professional theologically-trained teachers are not available). Lay teachers doubtless will continue to teach the youngest children. Putting such a plan into effect would require the cooperation of laymen both financially and in terms of understanding the pastor's revised role. Theological schools would have to devote much more time in their curriculum to the teaching of the future clergy-teachers.

Professor Fallaw is so confident of the possibilities in church education as he has outlined it that he sees pastor-teachers and supporting laymen actually engaging in " the launching of the second phase of the Second Protestant Reformation. Is not this the logical and necessary counter-part of the first phase, the revival of Biblical theology and the church? " [19] He apparently thinks the " first phase " to have been already achieved.

THE CHURCH PROVIDES NURTURE:

J. Donald Butler

Another writer who starts his consideration of Christian education with the church is J. Donald Butler. Dr. Butler formerly taught in Princeton Theological Seminary and the Presbyterian Theological Seminary in Austin, Texas, going then to Macalester College as chairman of the department of religion. His reputation as a theorist in this field was established by the publication of *Four Philosophies and Their Practice in Education and Religion.*[20] In 1962 his *Religious Education: The Foundations and Practice of Nurture* was published, designed as a textbook for survey courses in religious education. His first chapter in the latter book is especially germane to our present point. He calls it " The Church and Nurture." He begins his discussion of religious education with the actuality of the church as a phenomenon in the world, a " present fact " which makes it a spokesman in the world. He differentiates among the various New Testament figures of speech used to describe the church, concluding that " any understanding of the church necessarily has to be rooted in Christ who is the foundation of the church." [21] He then defines nurture as " an action (of the church, in the church) upon individuals so involving internal relationships that by it members are not just quantitatively or statistically added or quantitatively maintained in external relationship; they are made to have the kind of being that Christ has made possible to them and to become qualitatively more and more a part of his body. . . . It is an act of offering a gift. It is an overture or invitation to come in and participate in a partnership or community, and to enjoy it more fully." [22]

Butler, like the others whom we have considered in this chapter, rests his case for nurture squarely in the life of the church, whose essence must be understood. Without such a foundation of nurture theory in the church, he says, educational formulations for religion " may be without foundation and lacking in authenticity." [23]

9

Some British Perspectives

ALTHOUGH religious education theory is distinctively colored by local laws and cultural phenomena in each national setting, those nations which have a historic, cultural, and linguistic affinity for each other,[1] such as Great Britain and the United States of America, can profitably converse in recognizable symbols. The chief difference between England and the United States, of course, lies in the fact that England is technically a Christian nation, whereas technically the United States as state is neutral regarding religion. This difference is reflected in the fact that the Education Act of 1944 in Great Britain required the teaching of religion to be offered in the schools, along with a daily act of worship, whereas in the United States, as recent years have so clearly indicated, legal interpretations of the Supreme Court are constantly being sought in order to clarify the delicate line of demarcation between the state and religious expression and study.

Because of the long years of national involvement with religious establishment and the religious life in general, British theorists are numerous and vocal. Oftentimes they speak to their own countrymen in such a manner that overtones and undertones are missed by readers in other countries. At the same time, they often penetrate deeply into universal questions that pertain to the human situation in general. It is also illuminating to observe types of emphasis that have arisen in Great Britain in the decades under consideration in this study. In a sense this has been parallel to the American scene, and is not deeply influenced by the American theorists, or vice versa.

THE LIBERAL SPIRIT: A. *Victor Murray*

In Great Britain, liberalism, as we knew it in this country, was never quite so much the protestation of seekers after truth against the constrictions of restraint. In the United States, liberalism was generated in large measure by the need for intelligently informed minds, consonant with the spirit of the age, to break with the fundamentalism that had associated religion primarily with emotional evangelism. That, at least, was Horace Bushnell's necessity, and the movement he and his colleagues began was accelerated by the defensiveness of its foes.

In Great Britain the modern world emerged with *Sturm und Drang* also, but in a rather more sophisticated manner, and without any frontier psychology drumming up business for the defenders of hellfire and brimstone.

In recent decades it can be seen how the translation from the prevalent liberalism of the early part of the century into a more orthodox orientation was quite different in England from what happened in the Continent proper. Transitions went more smoothly. There was not so strong a consciousness of an acute break. In many ways American theology is more akin to German than to English theology in the sense that abrupt breaks and sudden shifts are much more pronounced here and in Germany.

So, for example, when A. Victor Murray's *Education Into Religion* was published in 1953, it sounded rather orthodox in contrast to writers like Chave, Bower, and Coe, who had been so long dominant in the American religious education scene. A rereading of Murray indicates that actually he manifested in this writing a most liberal outlook, but one couched in intellectually sensitive terms that sought not to slay the foe (if indeed he had any) so much as to describe him for what he was.

For example, although Coe had insisted that the educators ought to take over theology, so to speak, Murray more gently suggests that "doctrine . . . has to be treated 'educationally.' We are thinking beings and we must needs express our experiences in thoughts and the thoughts in words. It is also a necessity to be as exact as possible in the framing of these words, always remembering the different meanings of 'exactness' as in prose and poetry. Loose thinking, the use of shibboleths, half-truths and that parade of curious information which is the veneer of ignorance are an insult to human intelligence and work not to the glory of God. The fact that doctrine will not take us the whole way is no justification for not going with it as far as we can. But to use it as a substitute for Christian living, to exalt logical orthodoxy over against love and justice, to count obedience to authority superior to the plain movings of conscience is to fall into idolatry, substituting the name of the thing for the thing itself." [2]

Albert Victor Murray is an Oxford University man who went into the Student Christian Movement as a secretary from 1913 to 1922. During the next decade he was lecturer in education at the Selly Oak Colleges, Birmingham, after which, from 1933 to 1945, he was professor of education in the University of Hull. At the time of writing

Education Into Religion he was president of Cheshunt College, Cambridge. He is a Methodist, one who was honored by Dickinson College, Carlisle, Pennsylvania, with an honorary doctor of sacred theology degree in 1950. His writing has been prolific, including, among other major works: *Teaching the Bible: Especially in Secondary Schools* and *Natural Religion and Christian Theology.*[3]

Dr. Murray's liberalist position is evident in many ways throughout the book. He defines the goal of religious education as " a certain quality of life and a personal loyalty to Christ." Christianity is an attitude into which one grows.[4] He holds to an incarnational view of Jesus Christ, but this is interpreted in terms of Christ's " moral uniqueness." " What metaphysical uniqueness there may be is, and can only be, a matter of speculation, but it is worth noting that a metaphysical uniqueness such as would arise from a miraculous physical birth is not only undemonstrable but if it were demonstrated would neutralize His moral uniqueness." [5]

Murray regards the church as clearly " an integral part of the Gospel," but he opens the meaning of " church " to include many " who follow afar off." Insofar as the church is concerned with the diffusion of Christian principles and ideas in the world, these others are truly a part of the church set apart from any formal allegiances.[6] The Bible becomes the Word of God in that " it exhibits the search of man for God, and as they have searched they have not only found Him but also been found *of* Him." The divine nature of these writings is attested to in experience, which is the verification of their truth.[7] Doctrine is to be tested experientially also, for some doctrines merely reflect the particular circumstances under which they arose rather than reflecting universal validity.[8] " Truth," on the higher

levels, " is not a proposition but an experience." It is " in-
tuitively grasped." [9]

Professor Murray's interest in natural religion, which
expressed itself later in a whole volume on the subject, as
we have noted, comes out in *Education Into Religion* in
his suggestion that Christianity cannot be dissociated from
natural religion, the religion of all men. There is, as it
were, an overlapping of two circles, one representing
Christianity and the other representing natural religion.
The area of this overlap should be of tremendous concern
to Christian educators, for in that area lie questions per-
taining to mystery and existence. Religion is not primarily
an intellective matter, according to Murray. He seems to
reflect Schleiermacher in words like these: " The education of the emotions . . . is a most important aspect of
education into religion. Because religion is primarily feeling — a sense of the existence of the unseen world with
which we have to do — religious experience is akin far
more to aesthetic experience than to intellectual processes."

It was that kind of approach which seemed to many
American readers, who were becoming weary of the prag-
matist stress on problem solving, with all its intellectual
overtones, to sound a fresh note. Actually, psychologists
such as Allport and psychotherapists such as Tournier
were soon going to be saying similar things that would be
ingrafted into the newer existentialist Christian education, freed from liberalistic assumptions like Murray's
about natural religion, for example. These others were to
view man's " feelings " with equal attention, but as demon-
stration of what unregenerate man is like until his total
existence is redeemed into " the new Being."

THE PLATONIC STRAND: *Spencer Leeson*

Also liberal in spirit, but protected from the vagaries of liberalistic departures from historic theological understandings by his absorption in Anglican thought, was Spencer Leeson. At his death in 1956, Dr. Leeson was bishop of Peterborough, to which see he was appointed in 1949 after a distinguished career in church parochial and educational life. He served on the Board of Education of the Church of England, was headmaster of Merchant Taylor's School and Winchester College, lectured in the philosophy of religion at Southampton University College, and was rector of St. Mary's Parish, Southampton. He had served as canon of Chichester.

In 1944 he delivered the Bampton Lectures at Oxford University, later published (1947) as *Christian Education*. At the time Canon Leeson gave these lectures, there was great excitement in England, due to the passage by Parliament of the Education Act of 1944, which, as was mentioned above, contained certain religious provisions. Here we see his effort to provide an underlying rationale for Christianity's involvement in the educational life of the nation. Eight lectures are included in the published volume, some of which deals with technical, national, or local matters of little concern to overseas readers, but most of which is strictly in the realm of religious educational philosophy or theology.

Leeson saw a decline in a concerted effort to express educational understandings in mutually recognizable terms. In the postwar world the question as to what the nature of man is and what course he should follow is met only with " a confused amalgam of notions only half understood, derived from physical science, psychology, and sociology — evolution, relativity, self-expression, progress, and the like. Over all would hang a faint but genuinely held trust in a providential and directive power, who has benevolent intentions toward us but appears powerless to stop sorrow and misery."

Yet there are grounds for encouragement and hope; and in education as in other provinces of the spiritual life, we are waiting for a word. In many ways we are reminded in our own age of the spectacle presented by the first century of the Christian era. . . . Into all this came cutting clear the message of the Gospel, simplifying, raising, illuminating, purifying — and also directing. . . . So will it be again, for Jesus Christ is the same yesterday, today, and forever. . . . We must bend ourselves to master the currents and tendencies of so-called modern thought, not only at its higher levels but also in the exchange of the street and the market-place. We call for the aid of philosophy and scholarship; and if they are to be true helpers, they must never cheapen themselves, but yet in charity and sympathy and simplicity of spirit learn the language of the street and the fireside, so that they may be the possession of all God's children and not the closely-guarded treasure of a few.[10]

It will be observed from the foregoing that Leeson was philosophically oriented. This is accentuated in Lecture II, where he displays a great fondness for and dependence upon Platonic thought. " The reason why Plato's thought is so precious to a Christian student, is that in great measure he shares as a Christian in Plato's interpretation of human life." [11] The soul is thought to be of divine origin, maintaining a kinship with the divine in all its struggles and imprisonments. Balance and proportion are educational goals. The soul is likened in the *Phaedrus* to a chariot, pulled by the black horse of desire and the white horse of spirit. Who is the charioteer? None but reason. " By reason he [Plato] meant that which indeed should govern, the highest element in man's nature, recognizing its affinity with the divine and stirred by the vision of it to the noblest thought and action." [12] Growth is the normal habit of the soul. Leeson recognizes some of the time-bound limitations in Plato's thought, but by and large assumes that Platonic views are consonant with the Christian understanding. He lifts out Plato's central idea for education as this: " The sole and all-embracing purpose of man's life is to become as much like to God as possible." [13] He sees a continuity leading to fulfillment, Plato to Christ.

It has been remarked often that there is a strong Platonic stream in some types of Anglican theology.[14] Bishop Leeson surely represents that stream in its purest form. In the working out of this Christian idealism for education, he sees desirable a " fourfold alliance" among the home, the school, the state, and the church. " No single human being or collection of human beings should direct education. God made the child; and parent, state, school and church should regard themselves as his agents in its training — not balanced against each other in a precarious and mutually suspicious tension out of relation to any higher end, but as servants of God together and ministers of his purpose." [15]

THEOLOGICAL ROOTS OF EDUCATION:
M. V. C. Jeffreys

The phenomenon of the lay Christian who is theologically learned and articulate is a happy development within Protestantism during recent years. It has long been a tradition in Orthodox Church circles that laymen should be deeply immersed in theological work. Nicolas Berdyaev of our century is a case in point; or Nikos Nissiotis, an emerging younger theologian of the Greek Orthodox Church. We have referred above to Jacques Maritain, a distinguished lay theologian in the Roman Catholic Church. Montagu Vaughan Castleman Jeffreys belongs in this category, though his fame has unfortunately not carried far beyond his own country. Few Americans have read his works or met him. For some years he has been professor of education and director of the Institute of Education of the University of Birmingham, which means that he has supervisory responsibility over the teachers training colleges in an important part of the Midlands. Previously he was professor of education in Durham. He is a communicant of the Church of England.

Professor Jeffrey's books include three that are devoted directly to the question of theology in relation to education. In 1946 *Education: Christian or Pagan* was published, a volume in the series edited by W. R. Niblett, Educational Issues of Today. His thesis in that book is that " education is bound to be pagan unless it is Christian through and through, in purpose, content, and method." He addresses himself to the theme of " English Educational Ideals," pointing out the irony that though the assumption is that England's education is based on Christianity, actually this Christianity itself is so misunderstood by many leaders as to constitute a travesty of the " real article." [16] For example, much talk is done of "moral education," but the ideals concerning such are usually limited to the ethical field, even in so outstanding an interpreter as Sir Richard Livingstone, who refers to " that ultimate spiritual reality which we call God."

The truth is that, in spite of the European adoption of the Christian religion, the prevailing cultural tradition of the West has been Hellenic rather than biblical. To our Hellenic heritage we owe not only our belief in the self-sufficiency of human reason and virtue, and therefore our " ethical " view of religion and personal character, but also the divorce of an intellectual *élite* from the working life of the community and of " liberal " from " vocational " education. These social and cultural cleavages, traceable back to the Greek disparagement of manual labor and the assumption of an *élite* of free citizens, were greatly aggravated by the Industrial Revolution.[17]

That M. V. C. Jeffreys is therefore quite opposed to any " counterfeit " kinds of Christianity is patently clear. He cuts through all the subterfuges whereby essentially pagan cultural values have been " baptized " and seeks to establish Christian education on a strictly Biblical basis.

What are some of " the underlying assumptions of Christian education "? (1) Christianity is not so much a metaphysical or ethical system as " a way of dealing with situations." (2) Man is not to be regarded as a superior animal but as a sinful child of God. (3) Man cannot be adequately explained in terms of reason or nature. (4) Christianity is " not merely the statement of the law of love . . . but . . . the means by which obedience to that law can become possible." [18]

Glaucon: An Inquiry Into the Aims of Education (1950) is named after " Socrates' most faithful stooge in the *Republic*. He it is who follows the argument through to the end." [19] Jeffreys' burden in this book is to show that the supreme concern of education must be with persons, in freedom and in community. Modern forms of individualism and of collectivity are both denials of true personhood, which can appear only when seen in the context of relationship to God. " Perhaps the best way to waken in modern folks a sense of the meaning of religion is not to start with a discussion of God . . . but to help them to realize the religious nature of normal experience — the relation between love, creation, and freedom, and above all the meaning of redemptive love in personal relations, so that they can see that this is indeed the shape and pattern of the world — that life is like that. Then, when they see the Cross uplifted, they will recognize the true meaning of life." [20]

A third book is called *Beyond Neutrality: Five Essays on the Purpose of Education.*[21] Here he takes up similar themes, as he developed these for journal articles: education and belief, responsible choice, personal freedom — all characteristic questions which M. V. C. Jeffreys ponders with theological penetration and educational acumen.

10

A Measure of the Matter

THIS book began with the question proposed a quarter of a century ago by Harrison S. Elliott and the challenge thrown out to religious education theorists by H. Shelton Smith equally long ago. The intervening decades have produced an abundant harvest of materials in response to Professor Smith's challenge. Our purpose in this book has been to look at the types of religious education theory that have emerged during the period of reconstruction from 1940 to the present. We have isolated and examined eight types of approach to the church's contemporary teaching task, each based upon certain presuppositions of its own.

It would be an interesting exercise for students in a theological seminar to make a rather systematic investigation of these writers whom we have been discussing to see exactly how they " stack up " with regard to formal theological categories; for example, the doctrine of God, the nature of the person of Jesus Christ, the view of the church, etc. Comparative Christology, soteriology, hermeneutics, ecclesiology, and so on, can be effectively undertaken with small groups of writers in mind, provided that the students are patient enough to make careful tabula-tions of their own views and take the trouble to find out exactly what each writer is seeking to say. It is a rather more difficult task to do this with a group of writers in a field, say, like religious education, where the primary purpose of the authors is not to present theological *summae* but to work from others' presuppositions in theology (their churches' or their favorite theologians', with some of their own thrown in for good measure, perhaps). For in such a case, one works with reflected theological materials, which sometimes look quite different in the guise in which they appear than they would in somewhat different contexts. For example, Thomas Aquinas' ideas concerning bringing potentiality into actuality, translated into educational terms, can look very much like progressive education! Or, what in a strictly liberalist writer sounds like a universe open-ended to infinity may in reality be a God who works quite adamantly according to the principles of freedom whereby he tends to limit even himself! Well-nigh innumerable projects will occur to any seminary group in the theology or philosophy of religious education that might grow out of a consideration of these schools of educational thought within the religious community known as the Christian church.

For our present purpose, however, we are freed from such academic exercises. Instead, let us draw some observations of a more general nature out of our study.

A VARIED SPECTRUM

Certainly there must be an agreement that the types of theoretical formulation of the educational task of the church represent an interesting variety. Educators have never been famous for preferring a monochromatic *status quo.* In fact, they have often been innovators, pioneers, adventurers — sometimes even to the extent of being regarded as " dangerous characters." One remembers how the kindergarten, Friedrich Froebel's gift to the world which has outlasted those other " gifts " — the geometrical figures in which he put so much store — was regarded by the educational authorities in Prussia to be a downright suspiciously subversive scheme, and for a while was proscribed. In the church order of things, one remembers how clergymen in America first opposed the development of Sunday schools because these lay-operated and community-oriented " schools " gave promise of becoming a threat to the life of the parish churches, which, indeed, did happen in some cases. (Sunday school treasuries separate from the budget of the supporting parish are known to have survived in some cases even until now!)

If the response to H. Shelton Smith's challenge had been made only in terms of some committee that worked out the proper " new " answers, we can be sure that the result would have been infinitely less satisfying, in many ways, than the situation as it has actually developed. There has been a history of the pursuit of ecumenically acceptable statements of goals for Christian education, usually under the sponsorship of a council of churches whose committee rosters must compose adequate representation from the different churches, the several denominational boards, and the various parts of the country. Someone has said that one thing we can always thank God for is that *he* does not work by the committee method even though we think the church has to do so. This is not to be ungrateful for the many committees of the National Council of the Churches of Christ in the U.S.A. that have labored hard and long to produce some very satisfying statements indeed.[1] That is a stage *beyond* the level at which we have been thinking in this book. What happens, actually, is that the people who are assigned to work on such committees first read and discuss with their colleagues the ideas in the books of individual writers. It would be edifying to look at some of the group statements of purposes of Christian education to see how, indeed, they reflect the seminal ideas that the theorists have first presented.

How obviously, for example, the 1920's and 1930's confidence in a "progress" view of history was reflected in phrases formerly popular, such as, "building the Kingdom of God"; or how the less complicated views of human personality were reflected in references to "growing persons"; or how a "domesticated" type of theology preferred to talk of "the Fatherhood of God and the brotherhood of man." On the other hand, nowadays, the theological climate having changed considerably, there will be a tendency to talk of the divine initiative as being reflected in human society, of the judgment as well as the love of God, of the need for repentance and forgiveness prior to the educational efficacy of any system.

REFLECTIONS IN CURRICULUM

Although the quest still goes on for a cooperatively produced and ecumenically acceptable curriculum for the schools of the Protestant churches, it is not yet evident that any real agreements have been reached regarding this matter. The question that Iris Cully once raised and with which D. Campbell Wyckoff began his study *Theory and Design for Christian Education Curriculum,* "Is ecumenical curriculum possible?"[2] still has not been answered in the affirmative, in spite of such hopeful prospects as the new interdenominational curriculum outlines that have been in process for some years now.

One thing, however, *is* certain, and perhaps it is at this point that we should have more evident positive rejoicing: the ecumenical *theology* goes on apace — at least the ecumenical *theologizing*. Perhaps it was only in a day when naturalistically inclined religious educators envisioned a future time in which there would be a consensus based on their presuppositions (Elliott's thesis, in a slightly different perspective) that the effort to produce such curriculum made sense. Now it is evidently much more feasible to exploit for all it is worth the fact that Christians are learning to speak across boundaries in mutually recognizable symbols — to put the accent on theologizing, hoping that in due course this process will eventuate in a clarified educational mission for the church. At *that* point exciting things will happen which have not yet appeared.

Meanwhile, it is certainly true that the leading theorists considered in this book have indeed affected curriculum. *Christian Faith and Life* (The United Presbyterian Church U.S.A.) surely reflects James Smart's views, brought to a Biblical " fulfillment " under the even more stringent Scriptural views of his successor as editor in chief, Norman Langford. *The Seabury Series* not only reflects Randolph Miller's, Reuel Howe's, and David Hunter's views — they were instrumental in its development. The new curriculum of the Presbyterian Church in the U.S. (Southern), *Covenant Life,* and the new curriculum of the United Church of Canada show influences from a number of writers, certainly including Randolph Miller and Iris Cully, along with (in the case of *Covenant Life*) Rachel Henderlite, its editor in chief, whose earlier book *Forgiveness and Hope* sought to establish a theological rationale for education in the church. She has evinced a further theological interest in her 1964 publication, *The Holy Spirit in Christian Education.*[3] The United Church of Christ curriculum draws heavily on Lewis J. Sherrill and Reuel Howe, along with the theological formulations for education set forth by Roger L. Shinn (a professor of theology in Union Theological Seminary, New York) in *The Educational Mission of Our Church,* published in 1962.[4] Needless to say, fundamentalist or neo-evangelical curricula follow the guidelines laid down by such writers as Lois LeBar and Frank E. Gaebelein. The names widely known in connection with Beacon Press religious education publications are, of course, the very persons who have established the theoretical basis for that curricular approach: Sophia Lyon Fahs and Edith Hunter, in particular.

At the time of writing, not enough of The Methodist Church's new curriculum has seen the light of day to permit the searching light of criticism to find its intellectual parenthood, though one imagines that Harold DeWolf's hand will not be far absent from its foundations. The same reservation of analysis must hold for the new curriculum of the Lutheran Church in America, though it is known that Iris Cully has written one of the leadership training books for it, and we can see various neoorthodox aspects in the rationale as set forth in *As Christians Teach* by its editor in chief, Kent Gilbert.[5]

The chief impression elicited by mid-twentieth-century curriculum is a surprising similarity of feeling tone among the productions of the various mainstream denominations. Though denominational aspects still show through inevitably, there is a breakthrough of genuine theological seriousness and Biblical awareness. Methodologically, few even would consider being content with the old-fashioned

Herbartian approaches, save for an occasional fundamentalist press. There is evident a fruitful interaction between specific Christian content and a methodology derived from it that many thinkers have been exploring.

RELEVANCE IS TO SOMETHING

Although the word " relevance " has perhaps been overused in recent years, it cannot be denied that the word stands for a quality within the life of contemporary Christian experience and witness that had been lost for long and is now in the process of being rediscovered. The Christian faith is relevant *to* something — and that to which it is relevant is the human situation; to actual persons living in a real world; to mean, degraded, and needful souls in need of fellowship; to systems in need of radical reassessment and revision; to churches that have been more interested in promoting institutions or points of view than in being self-giving channels of the divine love of Christ.

It is this germaneness of the faith to persons and society as they are (and as they might be) which has constituted the renewal of the life of the church in all countries and cities. It is this which lies at the heart of the ecumenical movement, the liturgical renewal of the church, the catechetical revolution (characteristic alike of Roman Catholicism and Protestantism — and, interestingly enough, Judaism too).

Such relevance to real life invariably raises serious pedagogical questions. The richness of the recent decades' productiveness in theory reflects this growing concern and promises much for the work of the next several decades. One need only examine the nature of agenda at conferences of, say, The Religious Education Association nowadays. A comparison with those of previous years will show that a whole new era has dawned. Likewise, this can be seen in the journal of that association, *Religious Education*. In his last years, Coe and would lament in its pages that "theology" was again raising its lethal head. Now there has been for some years a joyful celebration of theology's rightful return to the religious education arena.

MUTUAL EXPLORING

One characteristic of the present period is the emergence of dialogue as a self-consciously sought after goal in religious education conversations. Consensus is not so much wanted (it was once considered the *sine qua non* of truth) as community, or rather, encounter in community. This does not mean that any kind of relativism has been settled for. In fact, the theological differences are sharper now than they were thirty years ago, and people are glad they are so. Now it is not necessary to apologize for believing strongly in something that a neighbor disbelieves in with equal fervor. The important thing is that we shall be able to speak in love, in and through, over and beyond, our disagreements. Only thus can there be honest "meeting."

At sessions of The Religious Education Association's chapter in Chicago in recent years the writer has been privileged to witness a new dimension to this dialogue: the inclusion in it, more actively and with complete candor, of Roman Catholic priests and teaching sisters, alongside Jewish rabbis and Protestant ministers and directors of religious education. They were not seeking least common denominators. They were not following any shibboleth of "brotherhood" or "sharing." They were honestly having theological discussion and even debate in the spirit of true search after meaning. Community already existed in their hearts and minds. That is why ideas could be faced without feelings of threat to anybody.

It is not yet evident that much cross-fertilization has taken place in terms of the mutual exploration of ideas through books, however. It is disappointing to realize that Hofinger can write on the catechetical movement without showing awareness of the books that have created a stirring within Protestant Christian education, and that few Protestant writers display familiarity with writings of people like Hofinger, Sloyan, or Jungmann. Nor do neo-evangelicals seem to read (except to reject) the neoorthodox to any extent, whereas neither do the others show adequate appreciation for the strivings within neo-evangelical orthodoxy toward an intellectual statement of an adequate pedagogy. Transverse dialogue is indicated as a desideratum. Here too, however, are signs of a breakthrough. Father Sloyan's recent volume on pastoral catechetics [6] has footnote references to Protestant kerygmatic theorists, specifically Iris Cully and Randolph Miller. *The Westminster Dictionary of Christian Education* contributors include a number of Roman Catholics and at least one Jewish writer. And Hakes's *An Introduction to Evangelical Christian Education* makes copious bibliographical references to " mainstream " Protestant writers.

TOWARD A HISTORICALLY–ORIENTED
PERSPECTIVE

It is to be hoped that our survey and classification of the types of religious education theory prevalent in the Christian church at this juncture of history will give us some possible clue as to a perspective on the whole educational task of the church. What shall we say to it? Is there any possibility of achieving a synthesis, or at least an underlying principle of unity?

It is this writer's suggestion that what these types show is that there is no such thing as *the* Christian education apart from the situational matrix in which the church develops its pedagogy from generation to generation. There is no doubt on the score of there being one gospel, one Lord and Savior Jesus Christ, one almighty God and Father of us all — these are affirmations of dogmatic theology generally agreed upon by all Christian bodies within the one body. But such dogmatic realities are taught by the church in its various branches according to the understanding of them in each given time and place. The methodology prevalent in any time and place will reflect those basic understandings also. *The Christian search for an education produces in any generation whatever kinds of education are required and indicated by the things most surely valued and believed in the various companies of those called Christian.* Even were the *corpus Christianum* once again manifested in external unity (and many scholars doubt if it existed in any degree comparable to what is sometimes alleged, even in the Middle Ages), there would be different theories of education depending on the stance within the body of Christendom from which a particular educational task needed to be viewed.

In the next chapter an effort will be made to set forth what seem to be some implications of this view that Christian education needs to be more aware of its historical foundations (diverse as these may be) and its potentialities in the light of historical dimensions.

11

Historical Dimensions
for Christian Education

P ERHAPS more than in any other aspect of the church's life and work in the twentieth century, the educational concern has been directed toward immediate needs and situations. In the past, however, this has been a quite different matter from the stress on "relevance" which we were discussing in the last chapter. "Presentism" was a major characteristic especially of the modern religious education movement shortly after the beginning of the twentieth century. The year 1903, as we have seen, was important, for in that year The Religious Education Association was founded. From that time on, fruitful contacts between religious and secular education led also to a kind of amalgamation of the secular and the religious from the side of the religious educators. Maybe this was a phase of the nascent sophisticating of religious education; a latecomer on the scene of the theological disciplines, it had to " go the limit," as it were.

Subsequent developments made it quite clear that from 1903 on, certain concerns and processes were to take over as regnant considerations during the following thirty years and more. That was the era H. Shelton Smith describes so carefully. Influenced by many parallel developments in the intellectual world, such as the pragmatic philosophy, views of progress, educational psychology, sociology, and also by the many ramifications of the liberalist theology, ranging from textual criticism to the social gospel, religious education people in pivotal positions tended to look toward a kind of pedagogical brave new world. They set the child in the midst; they concentrated on process as over against content. " Content " itself was reinterpreted in such a manner that the traditional theological categories often seemed irrelevant to the thinking through of pressing issues of particular times and places, local groups and classes and institutions. In making a broad statement like this, one is of course in danger of oversimplifying. If the child was made central, for example, he certainly deserved a chance at a central concern, having been neglected for many centuries *as* child. Nor can the religious education people be accused of having reached quick and easy means for giving him the kind of religious education they felt he needed. After all, he was a person, and as such he presented a rather complex phenomenon even to the psychology of the pre-" depth " days. But in the earlier part of this century, with its emphasis on fact-finding and the interpretation of data, hope was abundant that his character could indeed be molded into the understanding, rational creature modern religion expected him to become. He would, indeed, not so much be molded as " uncovered "; he could be assisted to reach the heights for which he was intended by the " creative process " that operated within his spirit. The advent of the " depth " psychologies, following Freud, was to alter some of the early optimism, and before World War II had become history, original sin loomed again as a live option for Christians who had pretty well abandoned it.

" PRESENTISM "

As we saw in Chapter 1, the " presentism " of religious education had found its chief spokesman in George Albert Coe. Using, perhaps, a cue from John Dewey (Coe never especially liked to be called a " disciple " of Dewey's), Coe put his major accent — one that was echoed for many years in every Protestant denomination — on *reconstruction:* " reconstruction, continuous reconstruction," viewed as the " essence of the divine work in and through the human." Coe admitted that " we cannot reconstruct anything unless we are acquainted with it; we cannot take a creative part in the moral order without intelligence as to its present and its past. But the focal point of true education is not acquaintance with the past, it is the building forth of a future different from the present and from the past. Moreover, creative education implies that the nature and the degree of this difference are to be determined within and by means of the educative processes; they cannot be dictated or imposed; they cannot be discovered by exegesis of any historical document." [1]

Certainly one would not want to argue for any avoidance of the importance of immediate experience. However, in restrospect, we can see that an experimental school of educational theory did tend to identify the subjective response of the growing person with the action of the Holy Spirit in such a manner that the Holy Spirit was more the projection of man's aspiration than the activity of the divine Lord. Coe had said that " learning to be a Christian " (from the learner's standpoint) " should be, essentially and primarily, an experience of free creativity." Whether such " free creativity " could be equated with the divine-human encounter of classical Christian thought eventually became doubtful. Parenthetically, however, we should note that recent existentialist interpretations of religious experience as being more properly " total involvement of the person's whole being " are giving rise to a much profounder evaluation of what might happen in a teaching-learning situation that is Christian in its dimensions. It is a little difficult to imagine that skill in building a Palestinian first-century village out of papier-mâché would be able to perform more than providing the child with a more interesting way to acquire knowledge about how a Palestinian village looked. If, however, situations can be devised in which the child's experience with classroom data can lead to an existential involvement with what it means to respond to Christ today, even as those in the first century had either to accept or reject him — experience understood existentially can indeed be a channel of religious learning.[2]

What I am suggesting here is that insofar as religious education confined itself to the experience of the moment or the evolving future, it was unnecessarily delimiting itself. It may be true, in one sense, as Lawrence Durrell says in *Justine*, that " we are the children of our landscape; it dictates behavior and even thought in the measure to which we are responsive to it." [3] But the landscape of Alexandria or any other city or moment of time is a complex of many things. It is scarcely a simple present or a yet unborn future. The fact seems to be that in any given moment of experience each person acts in relation to all that has happened to him heretofore. Furthermore, he is surrounded — in Christian understanding, at least — by a great cloud of witnesses. No person has only single, discrete experiences; one does not function experientially in a personal vacuum.

All that has happened — personally, familially, racially, nationally, historically — is party to his present exposure to experience.

THE CASE FOR HISTORY

This brings us to the matter of historical dimensions. For just as in the classroom situation we have frequently been aware of only the present ingredients of what we were doing, so in the larger field of educational theory we have often been content with a temporally limited field of vision. Much of twentieth-century functionalistic, progressivistic, and instrumentalist educational theory up to 1940 seems to have suffered from such a self-imposed limitation. Everyone was so terribly afraid of being in bondage to the shackles of the past that all sought to avoid the semblance of what was considered to be intellectual or spiritual slavery. Even the New Testament phrase the "reign of God" was thought by some to be inadequate for the modern world unless it was translated into "democracy of God." When, later, J. H. Oldham was to say that "real life is meeting," he did not mean anything like the divine-action-through-commission procedures!

It is noteworthy that since H. Shelton Smith uttered his now-famous challenge to religious educators back in 1941 (in his book *Faith and Nurture*) to reexamine their theological foundations, most of the constructive thinkers have departed from what we have implied was "naïve presentism," as we have seen. The earlier thinkers in this field were not intellectually naïve, however. Coe and his contemporaries had first-rate minds. They had intellectual power and thought consistently. Coe was thoroughly logical. If one eschews most of what has been done in theology in the past, then one must perforce put an emphasis on contemporary reconstruction, and for him this meant that the educators were to become theologians. That is, instead of taking his cues from dogmatic or systematic theology, the educator himself should be the maker of fresh theology as he goes along, so to speak. That was especially important if one believed, as Coe did, in salvation by the Christian education process itself.

It is especially at this point that the newer thinkers in Christian education theory have departed from the stream of Coe and others. They have been expressing a willingness to learn once more from the technical theologians. Because contemporary theologians have a historical approach to their field, there has appeared a slowly growing historical perspective on the educators' part. To be sure, some Christian education thinkers qua theologians (for they too are a part of the theological inquiry and rightly so) have chosen to take their stand on particular theological grounds, which involve a certain measure of preliminary definition. Thus Randolph Crump Miller defines theology as truth-about-God-in relation-to-man and James D. Smart insists on the primacy of the Scriptures " as the record of a revelation that is unique in our world." [4] Withal, the writers who have had the greatest influence in the constructive rethinking of Christian education foundations since H. Shelton Smith have been much more receptive to what the technical theologians have been saying, as well as open to the illuminative insights coming from contemporary thinking in other fields which have a bearing on the pedagogical task. Cross-disciplinary conversation is now an accepted mode of intellectual inquiry, and it is obviously going to continue to play a part in religious education theorizing.

A LARGER IDENTITY

An interesting thing has therefore been happening. Religious education has been rediscovering its identity with the total theological task of the Christian church. Two of the most potent influences in the theological world in recent decades are the revival of Biblical theology and the ecumenical movement. It is significant that in both of these the historical dimension has been uppermost, and this has been bound to affect educational thinking. The reemphasis on Biblical studies has brought scholars into new touch with history. Since God's revelatory actions were in historical events, no Biblical scholar could any longer avoid the necessity of thinking through the meaning of historical events. In Amos Wilder's words, we must deal with the " world story," beginning with Creation and running through " the calling and proving of Israel, the coming of the Messiah and the New Israel, on to the judgment and the new creation." " This story," he says, " had elements that could be called historical and others that were nonhistorical. Yet for the believer no part was mere chronicle; sober narrative and heavenly transactions belonged alike to this salvation drama." [5]

In the case of the ecumenical movement, practically every participating branch of the one church of Christ has had to reexamine its own historical roots and developments in order to communicate its self-understandings to sister communions. There has been some adverse criticism of the conferences on a worldwide scale in recent years of Methodists, Congregationalists, the Reformed churches, Lutherans, Anglicans, etc. Instead of being viewed as providing competition to the ecumenical movement proper, these may be considered only a necessary study of the denominational self-images in relation to the larger perspective of ecumenical oneness. What do Methodists in England, Australia, and the United States have in common apart from such sociological differences as that in England a Methodist minister may smoke but not drink, in Germany, drink but not smoke, but in the United States, he may do neither? What is Anglicanism in relation to the indigenous national churches that do not have any preferential establishment relationship with regard to their governments as Canterbury has at least with Her Majesty? Questions like these have projected theologians everywhere into historical inquiry. Technical ecclesiastical historians as such have contributed to this; they too are much more concerned about the uses of history than were their predecessors, who so often were content to be fact finders and chroniclers.

In a sense, theology is at one with history in general at this point. The exposure to the newer dimensions of historical scholarship has introduced an exciting aspect to every intellectual discipline that is sensitive to the necessity for continuous reinterpretation of every realm of human experience. One notes that even the slick magazines for business executives are developing this " angle." This is not the same thing as reconstruction of experience; it is, rather, looking at contemporary experience in the light of history in such a way that illumination will come even upon the *kinds* of questions we ask *about* our human experience.

The late R. G. Collingwood was speaking of this dimension when he wrote in *The Idea of History:*

In history, as in all serious matters, no achievement is final. The evidence available for solving any given problem changes with every change of historical method and with every variation in the competence of historians. . . . Every new historian, not content with giving new answers to old questions, must revise the questions themselves. . . . This is not an argument for historical skepticism. It is only the discovery of a second dimension of historical thought, the history of history: the discovery that the historian himself, together with the here-and-now which forms the total body of evidence available to him, is a part of the process he is studying, has his own place in that process, and can see it only from the point of view which at this present moment he occupies within it.[6]

Thus, the *kind* of history to which many contemporary Biblical scholars and technical theologians have been drawn is a history that pulsates with vitality, a living history that does not consist merely of lifeless, impersonal data, but a dynamic reality in which the present generation, including the historian himself, can actively participate.

Collingwood goes on to insist that since the historian can never possess empirical knowledge of his facts, what he must do is to "reenact the past in his own mind." Something of this quality is involved in the idea of historical remembrance, of which some writers speak, the re-presentation of past realities in such a manner that we become contemporaneous with them, and they with us. A notable example of this is the event of the Last Supper, a historical moment in which Jesus and his friends broke bread together in an upper room in Jerusalem. Every time the Christian community reenacts that event in the eucharistic meal of the church, we are transported back in time to that Last Supper; the Lord is present with us now as we break bread; and we are projected forward eschatologically to the heavenly banquet. Each of us who chooses to participate in this recollection in terms of present experience must make an act of personal decision as to what this means for him.

We can see in another way how this historical concern manifests itself. When we engage in discussions about doctrine, practice, beliefs — the raw material of every church school classroom, theological seminary lecture-discussion, or student bull session — we can be so deeply embroiled in the immediacy of our present debate that we lose sight of the fact that what makes our present conversation worthwhile at all is the realization that we are sharing now in the ongoing conversation that has characterized Christians ever since the first days of the church. We do not start *de novo* when we ask what life is about, what meaning our faith possesses, what the corridors of time signify, who Jesus was, what is the relevance of religion to life, and so on. Always we are in a great succession of the believers and doubters who have pondered these selfsame questions. The only difference between the first Christians and ourselves in this respect is that the intervening centuries have produced many more ideas and data than they had to deal with; for all that has happened in every century since then has become a part of our heritage too. It would be naïve to assume that our theological perspective must be or even could be a *tabula rasa* on which only new experience will be written. All that has been written there is part of us, insofar as we are exposed to it and are taught by it.

Protestants especially need to be reminded of the need for a historical perspective, since we so often allege freedom of interpretation to be the most essential Christian prerogative. The interpreters of the Christian religion in the liberal nineteenth century and after liked to think of themselves as moving into an ever freer and more refined air. Not only was there a desire to throw off the intellectual blinders; people in the church often wanted to repudiate everything that made the church seem to be antisecular; the whole thrust was to strengthen the identification of Christendom with the world at large in its finest aspects. Philosophies tended not to be derived from the gospel, but the gospel itself was transmogrified into philosophy. All that seems terribly dated now, of course. Few Christian thinkers any longer, except a few extreme "leftists," would prefer John Dewey's category of "the religious" to attachment to some specific religion, the latter of which he repudiated. Instead we have gone happily back into Biblical studies, into neo-Calvinism, neo-Lutheranism, etc. Even John Wesley is now being reexamined theologically and is coming out a better theologian than sometimes he was thought to have been. The result has been a gradual rediscovery of our various historical perspectives. But herein lies a potential theological myopia. Too often we talk as if our Christian faith began with the sixteenth or seventeenth century, or that if it did begin with the first century, nothing really much of significance happened between the fourth and the sixteenth centuries. It is sobering to realize that the Roman Catholic Church, though it did get rather indelibly colored by Thomas Aquinas and other medieval influences, nevertheless, in its comprehensive understanding of its own catholicity, has been able to embrace all centuries as its heritage.

SOME EDUCATIONAL IMPLICATIONS

Returning specifically to Christian education, let us make several observations as to what implications lie in our recovery of a historical dimension in that aspect of the church's life.

1. In respect to its scope as a theological discipline, Christian education will maintain an intellectual stature that it has deprived itself of by ignoring historical perspectives. Seminary students often have found religious education courses tedious to endure in comparison with theology, Bible, or even church history proper. In making this recommendation, I do not mean to suggest any crass departmental competition within the theological faculty, but only to highlight the apparent fact that theological students are attracted by the magnetic pull of ideological analysis rooted in historically illustrated data. As a matter of fact, before the revival of Biblical theology and the newer approaches to historical theology, sometimes it was the Bible and systematics departments that tended to be on the deadly dull side. It is no accident that religious education departments ascended in enrollment and influence in the period of the 1920's, for example, at the very time when deadly *Systematikers* held sway over the queen of the sciences and when textual analysis all but drained the Scriptures of any thrill. In those days the religious education people seemed exciting because they were at least daring. But in a time when theology once again reigns supreme, as she ought, and the Bible is once again viewed as an exciter to faith, as it properly should be, the situation is considerably different. The excitement of theology and Biblical studies is apparent even in sophisticated Ivy League colleges where a few years ago few ever ventured into anything except an occasional required religion course.

Religious education cannot be influential in helping to recover the teaching ministry of the church in its fullness unless there is a willingness to get beyond the stage of being a how-to-do-it laboratory. Emil Brunner did point out that many a person will go to heaven on account of his mastery of the " what " but to hell because of his failure in the " how." But Brunner was assuming a mastery of the " what " that will necessarily spill over into the pragmatic considerations of the " how." If the " how " is to rate as a theological discipline, it must be buttressed by thoughtful content and inquiry and a willingness to reckon with facts of historical development.

At innumerable points the curriculum in religious education can be strengthened. The motive should not be to compete with these other scintillant disciplines, but to learn from them, relate to them, and indeed, contribute to them as the communicative processes are explored. The subject matter of Christian education, covering so broad a sweep of human experience, can lead itself into fascinating intellectual stimulation for students.

The contemporary can be illuminated by the historical in Christian education theory. Here are a few illustrations.

Sometimes we have talked as if home-family relations with the church were a concern that only recently emerged as important to the Christian community. But when we look back we find Chrysostom telling parents about the right way for parents to bring up their children, and Cotton Mather, in his " Brief Essay to Direct and Excite Family Religion," writing in 1703:

I would make a proposal, for family meetings, to be so managed and ordered among us, that they may prove serviceable sacrifices in our families. It hath been a laudable custom, in many places, for a dozen families in a vicinity to combine into a design of meeting at each other's houses, at fit seasons, to spend an hour together, in prayers and psalms, and repetition of sermons, and religious conferences about the things of God. It would be a real service to religion, yea, and unto themselves also, if the pastors of our churches would animate and encourage such family meetings among their well-disposed people.[7]

We talk sometimes of the analysis of teaching methodology as something discovered in modern times, whereas back in the third century Gregory Thaumaturgus was already discussing the teaching methods of his master, Origen, in the catechetical school at Alexandria:

When he perceived anything that was not useless and unprofitable and ineffectual in us, he broke the ground, turned it over, watered it, used every device, applied all his skill and care, and wrought us into shape. The " thorns and thistles," and all the tribe of wild grasses and herbs which our mad and startled soul had sent forth and thrown up (for it was disordered and hasty) he cut out and pulled up with his inquiries and restraint, grappling with us in argument, and sometimes overthrowing us in true Socratic fashion if he espied us rushing off in all directions like wild horses.[8]

And Augustine in the early fifth century recognized individual differences in the persons whom the catechist was called upon to address, recommending that one must teach differently, depending on whether one is dealing with " a cultivated man, . . . a foreigner, a rich man, a poor man, a private citizen, a public man, a man set in some authority, a person of this or that nation, of this age or that, . . . a man representing this or that philosophical school, this popular and erroneous persuasion or the other." He also recognized that the teacher cannot avoid his own involvement in the situation, saying, " In sympathy with my own varying emotions my discourse itself starts, proceeds, and ends." [9]

The Sunday school is a mere nineteenth-century development, but across the years, long before Robert Raikes bequeathed the Sunday school to us, the church was inventing means peculiar to its task — the catechumenate, the catechetical school, the cathedral school, the university. Luther insisted that the magistrates get behind schools, and Charlemagne decreed as early as 802, " Laymen shall learn thoroughly the creed and the Lord's Prayer." Maybe Wesner Fallaw is right in suggesting that just now the time has come when the church should make another bold venture, not assuming that the Sunday school is the final possible answer to religious instruction as we plan church education for tomorrow.

Nor is Christian education just an American phenomenon. The national histories of every country into which Christendom has penetrated would provide seminar material for many a mind-stretching experience. And let us not forget that the precursors of the ecumenical movement were the interdenominational efforts and conferences in religious education; nor that the Division of Christian Education of the National Council of the Churches of Christ in the U.S.A. holds the copyright to the Revised Standard Version of the Scriptures!

2. A corollary of this is that insofar as Christian education as a discipline explores its historical roots, it would be able to enter into more fruitful dialogue with its sister disciplines in the curriculum. One form this might take would be more strenuous courses in the history of religious education. Fortunately, better materials are gradually becoming available for this kind of exploration. Lewis J. Sherrill started us off well with his *The Rise of Christian Education,* which, unfortunately, he was never able to extend beyond the medieval period. Robert Ulich has shown a sensitivity to the religious dimension of educational

thought.[10] But apart from exposing students to courses in educational history, there are other important reasons for doing this sort of thing. In conversations with theologians, well-informed Christian education people can help them to focus more attention upon the teaching ministries of the church as these have been manifested historically.

There is a need for more fruitful collaboration across disciplinary boundaries between theologians and educators. I remember some twenty years ago how a group of religious education people and some theologians sat down together to talk about mutual intersections of their fields. They got nowhere. It was not entirely the fault of the educators, though admittedly they were doing precious little reading in theology at that time. But it was equally true that the theologians had done practically no reading in religious education. We can hardly expect them to become child development specialists or know how to operate group dynamics laboratories, but they should know that scholarly books have been written in the last fifteen years that merit any theologian's attention. What I am suggesting is that it is just as important for the Biblical and theological people to know the educational writings as it is for religious education people to know the theological books. Their mutual conversation would be further enriched if they could both have in the back of their minds the contributions of a person like Comenius, a bishop of the Unitas Fratrum and therefore important in church history, but also author of *The Great Didactic*, and because of his pedagogy sometimes called the " father of modern education "; or Thomas Aquinas not only as the author of the *Summa Theologica*, and therefore a great theologian, but also the architect of an educational theory whose influence extends to even so " modern " a phenomenon as

"Great Books" discussions, and guides the most power-
ful single church in Christendom; or Luther not merely as
the father of the German Reformation but also the insti-
gator of what ultimately became free universal education
in America and elsewhere.

3. A third implication is this: the church's practical
work in the world will be strengthened insofar as those
responsible for its teaching are able to arrive at the distinctive roots of its teaching. It is notorious that heresy
after heresy from the ancient past looms freshly in each
generation as if it were being presented to the world newly
conceived. Now, a little heresy is not a dangerous thing;
in fact, the church grows stronger whenever it is able to
combat a heresy constructively. But that is a different
thing from letting purely secular norms take over, or for
religious leaders to assume, even in the name of good-
will, that the theological dimensions ought to be soft-
pedaled or submerged. The church lost higher education,
for all practical purposes, when in the name of universal-
isms of various kinds it surrendered the ivy halls to secular
standards exclusively. The presence of a denominational
executive or a clergyman or two on a board of trustees
does little. I am not arguing for a return to a church-dom-
inated society. But I am urging that we ought to be at
least historically sophisticated enough to recognize the
difference between God presented as the "great valuer of
persons," or the "principle of concretion in the universe,"
and the God who is Father of our Lord and Savior Jesus
Christ. Shades of Pascal! The least that the teachers of
the church can do for our people is to help them *differentiate* among the principalities and powers of this world.
For, as our Lord prayed, we were not meant to be kept
from the world, but from the evil one. The Christian wit-

ness is to and in the world; it is never a mere reflection *of* the world. Teachers who know of the long centuries of development of the church's involvement with the world in and through education will be sensitive to these differences.

4. Finally, an acquaintance with the historical dimension will enable Christian education to sense both the wonderful variety of the past as heritage and the still unconquered realms of darkness against which the Holy Spirit ever contends. History gives us some keys with which to unlock some seeming mysteries. Why has the church tried again and again in a multitude of complex institutional forms to do a task whose outline is seemingly so simple and so clear? Why has the gulf between Athens and Jerusalem seemed at times to be bridged successfully and at other times merely to be widened? Why has there seldom been unity and concord between those who stress God's objective deed and those who emphasize man's subjective response? What is the relation of Christ to culture? Christ to the state? Christ to the divided entity which, though guilt-ridden about its fragmentariness, refuses to let him restore the unity for which it prays? What is the relation of the church's teaching task to questions like these, as well as many more? We shall be saved from vast anxiety and not a little self-confidence in our own prowess to form the world for Christ, when, through the eyes of history, we are able to discern in faith that it is not the church itself that has been the real teacher ultimately, but God the Holy Spirit, who has been forming us for his own ends.

Some persons fear that a concern with history on the part of Christian education might lead to obstructionism or a lack of relevance to the " nowness " of present experience. Actually by holding such a fear they may be only trying to set up a blockade against the divine initiative. Though man may indeed be subject to " time-conditioned habits and modes of thought " — and indeed we are all children of our particular city in time and space — yet in a very real sense we belong to all cities and all times. The Lord's call to us is basically the same as his call to the generations before us. How they responded and what they wrought are essential for our understanding as to how we should respond and what we might do for him. But the Christian educator, as historian, will only be able to do this when with alacrity, imagination, and not a little research, he is able, in Collingwood's words, to " re-enact the past in his own mind." [11]

Notes

PREFACE

1. The question, "Is ecumenical curriculum possible?" asked by Iris V. Cully in *Religion in Life* (Summer, 1960, pp. 426–433), with which D. Campbell Wyckoff opens his *Theory and Design of Christian Education Curriculum* (The Westminster Press, 1961, p. 15), still remains essentially unanswered. It should also be pointed out that it is only very slowly that the World Council of Churches has become involved in specifically educational questions, as evidenced by a few conversations at the Ecumenical Institute in Celigny. There is as yet no strong upsurge of concern to bring about an integration of the World Council of Christian Education and Sunday School Association with the World Council of Churches, as has been accomplished in the case of the International Missionary Council.

1. A QUESTION AND A CHALLENGE

1. Paul H. Vieth, ed., *The Church and Christian Education* (The Bethany Press, 1947).

2. William Clayton Bower, "Recent Trends in Christian Education: An Appraisal," *Religious Education,* Vol. LV, No. 4 (July–Aug., 1960), p. 243. Professor Bower was replying to my article, "Two Decades of Thinking Concerning Christian Nurture," *Religious Education,* Vol. LIV, No. 6 (Nov.–Dec., 1959), pp. 481–489. This chapter is based somewhat on material from that article and is used here by permission of the publisher, The Religious Education Association.

3. Harrison S. Elliott, *Can Religious Education Be Chris-*

tian? (The Macmillan Company, 1940), p. 9. For a recent, thorough study of Elliott, cf. Frederick Nile Harper, *The Thought and Work of Harrison S. Elliott* (unpublished Ed. D. project, Teachers College, Columbia University, 1964).

4. *Ibid.*, p. 10.

5. *Ibid.*, p. 319.

6. *Ibid.*, p. 310.

7. *Ibid.*, p. 312.

8. *The Journal of Religion*, Jan., 1941.

9. H. Shelton Smith, *Faith and Nurture* (Charles Scribner's Sons, 1941), p. vii.

10. *Ibid.*, pp. viii f.

11. H. Shelton Smith, "Christian Education," *Protestant Thought in the Twentieth Century*, ed. by Arnold S. Nash (The Macmillan Company, 1951), pp. 242–245.

12. Albert C. Outler, "H. Shelton Smith: An Appreciative Memoir," *A Miscellany of American Christianity*, ed. by Stuart C. Henry (Duke University Press, 1963), p. 17. In that essay Professor Outler alleges that *Faith and Nurture*, lacking a sequel by Professor Smith, has had no other sequel. "Christian nurture still awaits its still needed theoretical re-evaluation" (p. 13). Actually, though it is indeed regrettable that Professor Smith did not himself essay further work in this area, the fact is that his work spearheaded the entire reconstructive task, at least in the United States, as is reflected in this study.

13. Cf. "Theology and Christian Education," by James Blair Miller, *The Westminster Dictionary of Christian Education*, ed. by Kendig Brubaker Cully (The Westminster Press, 1963), pp. 665–668. See also George M. Schreyer, *Christian Education in Theological Focus* (Christian Education Press, 1962), esp. Chs. 1–3.

14. D. Campbell Wyckoff uses this alliterative series of " w " adjectives in *Theory and Design of Christian Education Curriculum*, as on p. 157. "What is the worshipping, witnessing, working community of the people of God? "

2. The Liberalist Continuum

1. David W. Jewell, "Liberalism," *The Westminster Dictionary of Christian Education*, pp. 389–392.

2. *Ibid.*, pp. 390 ff.

3. Smith, "Christian Education," *Protestant Thought in the Twentieth Century*.

4. Dorothy Tilden Spoerl, "Unitarian Universalist Association," *The Westminster Dictionary of Christian Education*, p. 681.

5. Sophia Lyon Fahs, *The Old Story of Salvation* (Beacon Press, Inc., 1955), p. viii.

6. *Ibid.*, p. xiv.

7. Sophia Lyon Fahs, *Today's Children and Yesterday's Heritage* (Beacon Press, Inc., 1952). The book has an introduction by Angus H. MacLean, The Theological School, St. Lawrence University. For a related point of view see Edith Fisher Hunter, *The Questioning Child and Religion* (Starr King Press, 1956); also Ernest J. Chave, *A Functional Approach to Religious Education* (The University of Chicago Press, 1947).

8. Cf., e.g., the title of A. J. William Myers' book, *Teaching Religion Creatively* (Fleming H. Revell Company, 1932). Recently a similar choice of title has been made in the instance of *Creative Teaching in the Church* by Eleanor Shelton Morrison and Virgil E. Foster (Prentice-Hall, Inc., 1963).

9. Cf. Iris V. Cully, *The Dynamics of Christian Education* (The Westminster Press, 1958), p. 141.

10. Fahs, *Today's Children and Yesterday's Heritage*, p. vii.

11. *Ibid.*, p. 15

12. *Ibid.*, p. 16.

13. *Ibid.*, pp. 21 f.

14. *Ibid.*, p. 181.

15. *Ibid.*, pp. 16 f.

16. *Ibid.*, pp. 164 f.

17. *Ibid.*, p. 8.

18. *Ibid.*, p. 29.

19. See also Sophia Lyon Fahs, and Elizabeth M. Manwell, *Consider the Children — How They Grow*, rev. ed. (Beacon Press, Inc., 1951).

20. Harry C. Munro, *Protestant Nurture: An Introduction to Christian Education* (Prentice-Hall, Inc., 1956), p. v.

21. *Ibid.*

22. *Ibid.*, pp. 8 ff.

23. *Ibid.*, p. 11.

24. *Ibid.*, p. 17.

25. *Ibid.*, p. 19.

26. *Ibid.*, p. 20.

27. *Ibid.*, pp. 23 f. The famous Coe "Coda" is contained at the end of *What Is Christian Education?* (Charles Scribner's Sons, 1929), p. 296, and is reproduced in *Basic Writings in Christian Education*, ed. by Kendig Brubaker Cully (The Westminster Press, 1960), p. 338.

28. *Ibid.*, p. 47.

29. *Ibid.*, pp. 63 f.

30. *Ibid.*, p. 262.

31. L. Harold DeWolf, "Neoliberalism," *The Westminster Dictionary of Christian Education*, pp. 460 f.

32. DeWolf, *Teaching Our Faith in God* (Abingdon Press, 1963).

33. *Ibid.*, pp. 124 f.

3. Psychologically-oriented Nurture

1. See Kendig Brubaker Cully, "Herbart, Johann Friedrich," *The Westminster Dictionary of Christian Education*, pp. 304 f.

2. See Earl A. Loomis, Jr., "Psychology, Depth," *The Westminster Dictionary of Christian Education*, pp. 531–532.

3. Cf. Roger Lincoln Shinn, *The Educational Mission of Our Church* (United Church Press, 1962).

4. Reuel L. Howe, *Man's Need and God's Action* (The Seabury Press, 1953).

5. *Ibid.*, pp. 8 f.

6. *Ibid.*, pp. 15 f.

7. Paul Tillich, *Systematic Theology*, Vol I (The University of Chicago Press, 1951), p. 8; cf. Reuel L. Howe, "Correlation, Principle of," *The Westminster Dictionary of Christian Education*, pp. 152 ff.

8. Howe, *op. cit.*, p. 50.

9. *Ibid.*, pp. 50 ff.

10. *Ibid.*, p. 57.

11. *Ibid.*, p. 101.

12. *Ibid.*, p. 106.

13. Treasure, Anthony P., in *ACU News*, Nov.–Dec., 1954, pp. 2 and 4. Published by the American Church Union, an organization devoted to Anglo-Catholic viewpoints.

14. Reuel L. Howe, *Herein Is Love* (The Judson Press, 1961); *The Creative Years* (The Seabury Press, 1959); *The Miracle of Dialogue* (The Seabury Press, 1963).

15. *Pastoral Psychology*, Feb., 1960.

16. Roy W. Fairchild, "The Contribution of Lewis J. Sherrill to Christian Education," *Religious Education*, Vol. LIII, No. 5 (Sept.–Oct., 1958), pp. 403–411.

17. *Ibid.*, pp. 403 f.

18. Lewis Joseph Sherrill, *The Gift of Power* (The Macmillan Company, 1955), pp. 68 ff.

19. *Ibid.*, p. 77.

20. *Ibid.*

21. *Ibid.*, pp. 110 ff.

22. *Ibid.*, pp. ix f.

23. Cf. Allen F. Bray, III, *The Return to Self-concern* (The Westminster Press, 1964), for further discussion of the concept of selfhood in Christian education.

24. Other books of Sherrill's not referred to in the preceding notes: *The Opening Doors of Childhood* (The Macmillan Company, 1939); *The Rise of Christian Education* (The Macmillan Company, 1944); *The Struggle of the Soul* (The Macmillan Company, 1951); *Guilt and Redemption*, rev. ed. (John Knox Press, 1957).

4. Education Through Relationship

1. Randolph Crump Miller, "Relationship Theology," *The Westminster Dictionary of Christian Education*, p. 563.

2. Martin Buber, *I and Thou*, 2d ed., tr. by Ronald Gregor Smith (Charles Scribner's Sons, 1958). For an extensive interpretation of Buber, see Maurice S. Friedman, *Martin Buber: The Life of Dialogue* (The University of Chicago Press, 1955).

3. Martin Buber, *Between Man and Man*, tr. by Ronald

Gregor Smith (Beacon Press, Inc., 1955), pp. 22 f.

4. *Ibid.*, p. 31.

5. These two essays were brought out in the United States in 1955 under the title of the larger collection of essays, *Between Man and Man.*

6. *Ibid.*, p. 83.

7. *Ibid.*, p. 85.

8. *Ibid.*, p. 91.

9. *Ibid.*, p. 96.

10. *Ibid.*, p. 101.

11. *Ibid.*, p. 113.

12. *Ibid.*, p. 116.

13. Randolph Crump Miller, *The Clue to Christian Education* (Charles Scribner's Sons, 1950), pp. vii f.

14. Randolph Crump Miller, *Biblical Theology and Christian Education* (Charles Scribner's Sons, 1956), p. viii.

15. *Education for Christian Living,* rev. ed. (Prentice-Hall, Inc., 1963); *Your Child's Religion* (Doubleday & Company, Inc., 1962).

16. Randolph Crump Miller, *The Clue to Christian Education,* p. 15.

17. *Ibid.*, p. 5.

18. *Ibid.*, p. 7.

19. *Ibid.*, p. 8.

20. *Ibid.*, p. 9.

21. *Ibid.*, p. 36.

22. *Ibid.*, pp. 107 f.

23. *Ibid.*, Ch. 8, pp. 120–137.

24. Miller, *Biblical Theology and Christian Education,* p. 4.

25. Bernhard W. Anderson, *The Unfolding Drama of the Bible* (Association Press, 1953), p. 12.

26. Miller, *Biblical Theology and Christian Education,* p. 18.

27. *Ibid.*, p. 117.

28. *Ibid.*, pp. 145 f.

29. See Howard Grimes, *The Church Redemptive* (Abingdon Press, 1958); *The Rebirth of the Laity* (Abingdon Press, 1962).

30. Randolph Crump Miller, *Christian Nurture and the Church* (Charles Scribner's Sons, 1961), p. 195.

31. *Religious Education,* 1962.
32. David R. Hunter, *Christian Education as Engagement* (The Seabury Press, Inc., 1963), p. 7.
33. *Ibid.,* p. 8.
34. *Ibid.,* p. 9.
35. Ibid., p. 47 f.

5. BIBLICAL BASES OF NURTURE

1. Roger L. Shinn, "Neoorthodoxy," *The Westminster Dictionary of Christian Education,* pp. 461 ff.
2. *Ibid.,* p. 463.
3. James D. Smart, *The Teaching Ministry of the Church* (The Westminster Press, 1954).
4. *Ibid.,* p. 10.
5. J. Stanley Glen, *The Recovery of the Teaching Ministry* (The Westminster Press, 1960).
6. Smart, *op. cit.,* pp. 19 f.
7. *Ibid.,* p. 38. *The Role of the Bible in Contemporary Christian Education* by Sara Little (John Knox Press, 1961), discusses Smart, Miller, and Sherrill, especially, as regards their understandings of the place of the Bible in the story of Christian nurture, against the background of the thought of the theologians William Temple, Karl Barth, Paul Tillich, Emil Brunner, and H. Richard Niebuhr. Dr. Little's book is an important contribution to the elucidation of this phase of recent thinking.
8. *Ibid.,* p. 108.
9. *Ibid.,* pp. 206 f.
10. Ralph D. Heim, *Religious Education,* Vol. L, No. 1 (Jan.–Feb., 1955), p. 71.
11. Howard Grimes, *The Journal,* Perkins School of Theology, 1955.
12. Hunter, *op. cit.,* p. 10.
13. Smart, *op. cit.,* p. 9.
14. James D. Smart, *The Interpretation of Scripture* (The Westminster Press, 1961); *The Creed in Christian Teaching* (The Westminster Press, 1962); *The Rebirth of Ministry* (The Westminster Press, 1960).
15. George F. Kneller, "Existentialism," *The Westminster*

Dictionary of Christian Education, p. 245. See also his *Existentialism and Education* (Philosophical Library, Inc., 1958).

16. *Ibid.,* p. 247.

17. Iris V. Cully, *op. cit.,* p. 10.

18. *Ibid.,* p. 9.

19. *Ibid.,* p. 35.

20. *Ibid.,* p. 76.

21. *Ibid.,* p. 86.

22. *Ibid.,* pp. 114, 118.

23. *Ibid.,* p. 119.

24. *Ibid.*

25. Ibid., pp. 129 ff., *passim.*

26. *Ibid.,* pp. 141 f.

27. *Ibid.,* p. 143.

28. *Ibid.,* pp. 146 ff.

29. *Ibid.,* pp. 147 ff.

30. *Ibid.,* p. 153.

31. Ch. 8, pp. 157–177.

32. Iris V. Cully, *Children in the Church* (The Westminster Press, 1960).

33. *Pastoral Psychology Book Club Preview,* March, 1960.

34. Iris V. Cully, *Imparting the Word: The Bible in Christian Education* (The Westminster Press, 1962).

35. *Ibid.,* p. 14.

36. Cully, *The Dynamics of Christian Education,* pp. 29 f.

37. D. Campbell Wyckoff, *The Task of Christian Education* (The Westminster Press, 1955), p. 18.

38. *Ibid.,* p. 23.

39. *Ibid.,* p. 82.

40. D. Campbell Wyckoff, *The Gospel and Christian Education* (The Westminster Press, 1959), p. 7.

41. *Ibid.,* pp. 111 f.

42. George Herbert Betts, *The Curriculum of Religious Education* (Abingdon Press, 1924), and William Clayton Bower, *The Curriculum of Religious Education* (Charles Scribner's Sons, 1925), were the previous " standard " works on the subject.

43. Wyckoff, *Theory and Design of Christian Education Curriculum,* p. 119.

6. Fundamentalism and Neo-Evangelicalism

Carl F. H. Henry, "National Association of Evangelicals," *The Westminster Dictionary of Christian Education,* pp. 445 f.

2. Gabriel Hebert *Fundamentalism and the Church* (The Westminster Press, 1957), pp. 18 ff.

3. N. B. Stonehouse, *J. Gresham Machen: A Biographical Memoir* (Wm. B. Eerdmans Publishing Company, 1954), pp. 336 ff.

4. *Revelation and the Bible: Contemporary Evangelical Thought,* ed. by Carl F. H. Henry (Baker Book House, 1958), p. 8.

5. The term "fundamentalist" has a different connotation in England from what it has in the United States. See, e.g., what it connotes within the Church of England situation, as discussed in *The Word of God and Fundamentalism* (London: Church Book Room Press, 1961), the addresses given at the Oxford Conference of Evangelical Churchmen, Sept. 1960.

6. H. W. Byrne, *A Christian Approach to Education: A Bibliocentric View* (Zondervan Publishing House, 1961), p. 6. A recent book dealing with perspectives on this area is *An Introduction to Evangelical Christian Education,* ed. by J. Edward Hakes (Moody Press, 1964). Among the contributors are Carl F. H. Henry, Harold Carlton Mason, Frank E. Gaebelein, C. E. Eavey, Cornelius Jaarsma, Lois E. LeBar, Henrietta C. Mears, C. Adrian Heaton, and Mark Fakkema.

7. Lois E. LeBar, *Education That Is Christian* (Fleming H. Revell Company, 1958), p. 5.

8. *Ibid.,* p. 21.

9. *Ibid.,* in Ch. III.

10. *Ibid.,* Ch. V, pp. 119–133.

11. *Ibid.,* pp. 187 ff.

12. *Ibid.,* pp. 232–239.

13. *Ibid.,* p. 241.

14. *Ibid.,* p. 31 ff.

15. Frank E. Gaebelein, *Christian Education in a Democracy: The Report of the N.A.E. Committee* (Oxford University Press, Inc., 1951).

16. *The Church and Christian Education*, ed. by Paul H. Vieth.

17. *An Introduction to Evangelical Christian Education.* (See note 6); *Religious Education: A Comprehensive Survey,* ed. by Marvin J. Taylor (Abingdon Press, 1960).

18. Gaebelein, *op. cit.*, p. 5.

19. *Ibid.*, p. 18.

20. *Ibid.*, pp. 24 ff.

21. *Ibid.*, p. 40.

22. *Ibid.*, pp. 157 ff.

23. *Ibid.*, pp. 274 ff.

24. See, e.g., the writings of Jerome and John Chrysostom. Cf. *Basic Writings in Christian Education*, pp. 41–61.

25. Gaebelein, *op. cit.*, pp. 289 f.

26. *Ibid.*, pp. 291 f.

27. Frank E. Gaebelein, *The Pattern of God's Truth: Problems of Integration in Christian Education* (Oxford University Press, Inc., 1954), p. v.

28. *Ibid.*, pp. 8 f.

29. *Ibid.*, pp. 21 ff.

30. *Ibid.*, pp. 48 ff.

31. *The Journal*, Perkins School of Theology.

32. *Contemporary Evangelical Thought*, ed. by Carl F. H. Henry (Channel Press, 1957), pp. 168–177.

33. *Fundamentals in Christian Education*, ed. by Cornelius Jaarsma (Wm. B. Eerdmans Publishing Company).

7. Ferment Within Roman Catholicism

1. Mary Helen Mayer, *The Philosophy of Teaching of St. Thomas Aquinas* (The Bruce Publishing Company, 1929).

2. Pierre Ranwez, S.J., " General Tendencies in Contemporary Catechetics," *Shaping the Christian Message*, abridged ed., ed. by Gerard S. Sloyan (Paulist Press; Deus Books, 1963), pp. 119 f.

3. *Ibid.*, pp. 125 f.

4. *Teaching All Nations: A Symposium on Modern Catechetics*, ed. by Johannes Hofinger, S.J., tr. by Clifford Howell, S.J. (Herder and Herder, Inc., 1961).

5. *Ibid.*, p. 388.

6. *Ibid.*

7. *Ibid.*, p. 390.

8. *Ibid.*, pp. 394–400.

9. Terence P. McLaughlin, C.S.B., " On the Christian Education of Youth," *The Church and the Reconstruction of the Modern World: The Social Encyclicals of Pius XI* (Doubleday & Company, Inc.; Image Books, 1957), p. 78.

10. *Ibid.*, p. 79.

11. *Ibid.*, pp. 79 f.

12. *Ibid.*, p. 82.

13. *Ibid.*, p. 83.

14. *Ibid.*, p. 87.

15. *Ibid.*, pp. 88 ff.

16. *Ibid.*, p. 106.

17. Cf. H. Richard Niebuhr, *Christ and Culture* (Harper & Row, Publishers, Inc., 1951).

18. McLaughlin, *op. cit.*, p. 107.

19. Gustave Weigel, S.J., " The Significance of Papal Pronouncements," *The Papal Encyclicals in Their Historical Context*, ed. by Anne Fremantle (G. P. Putnam's Sons, 1956), pp. 9–20, *passim.*

20. Johannes Hofinger, S. J., *The Art of Teaching Doctrine: The Good News and Its Proclamation* (University of Notre Dame Press, 1957), pp. 1 f. Another significant recent book is edited by Johannes Hofinger and Theodore C. Stone: *Pastoral Catechetics* (Herder and Herder, Inc., 1964). It includes essays by Gerard S. Sloyan, Bernard Cooke, Andrew M. Greeley, Sister M. Carol Frances, and others.

21. *Ibid.*, p. 8.

22. *Ibid.*, p. 11.

23. *Ibid.*, p. 19.

24. *Ibid.*, pp. 26 ff.

25. *Ibid.*, p. 39.

26. *Ibid.*, pp. 42 ff.

27. *Ibid.*, p. 243.

28. *The Education of Man: The Educational Philosophy of Jacques Maritain*, ed. by Donald and Idella Gallagher (Doubleday & Company, Inc., 1962).

29. Jacques Maritain, *Education at the Crossroads* (Yale University Press, 1943), p. 1.

30. *Ibid.*, p. 2.

31. *Ibid.*, pp. 2–28, *passim.*

32. *Ibid.*, pp. 39–51, *passim.*

33. *Ibid.*, pp. 88–118, *passim.*

8. Accent Upon the Church

1. Howard Grimes, *The Church Redemptive,* pp. 32–33, 34.

2. *Ibid.*, pp. 56, 57.

3. *Ibid.*, pp. 75, 79.

4. *Ibid.*, pp. 89–104, *passim.*

5. *Ibid.*, pp. 161.

6. Howard Grimes, *The Rebirth of the Laity,* Chs. 4, and 5, pp. 66–105.

7. *Ibid.*, p. 170.

8. Dora P. Chaplin, *Children and Religion,* rev. ed. (Charles Scribner's Sons, 1961), p. ix.

9. Dora P. Chaplin, *The Privilege of Teaching: Its Dimension and Demand for All Who Teach the Christian Faith* (Morehouse-Barlow Co., 1962), p. 103.

10. Dora P. Chaplin, " Preparation for the Sacramental Life," *Living Thankfully,* ed. by Harold R. Landon (The Seabury Press, 1961).

11. Chaplin, *The Privilege of Teaching,* pp. 70 f.

12. *Ibid.*, p. 56.

13. *Ibid.*, pp. 63 ff., *passim.*

14. Wesner Fallaw, *The Modern Parent and the Teaching Church* (The Macmillan Company, 1946).

15. Wesner Fallaw, *Church Education for Tomorrow* (The Westminster Press, 1960), p. 22.

16. *Ibid.*, p. 25.

17. *Ibid.*, p. 31.

18. *Ibid.*, pp. 51–52.

19. *Ibid.*, p. 205.

20. J. Donald Butler, *Four Philosophies and Their Practice in Education and Religion,* rev. ed. (Harper & Row, Publishers, Inc., 1957).

21. J. Donald Butler, *Religious Education: The Foundations*

and Practice of Nurture (Harper & Row, Publishers, Inc., 1962), p. 19.

22. *Ibid.*, p. 21.

23. *Ibid.*, p. 22.

9. Some British Perspectives

1. Cf. Kendig Brubaker Cully, "In Each Country," *The Teaching Church* (United Church Press, 1963), pp. 20–32, for a brief discussion of the national settings that must be reckoned with in Christian education.

2. A. Victor Murray, *Education Into Religion* (Harper & Row, Publishers, Inc., 1953), p. 151.

3. Murray's other writings include: *Teaching the Bible, Especially in Secondary Schools* (Cambridge University Press, 1955); *Natural Religion and Christian Theology* (London: James Nisbet & Co., Ltd., 1956); *The State and Church in a Free Society* (Cambridge University Press, 1958).

4. Murray, *Education Into Religion*, p. v.

5. *Ibid.*, p. 219.

6. *Ibid.*, p. 181.

7. *Ibid.*, p. 59.

8. *Ibid.*, pp. 145 ff.

9. *Ibid.*, p. 173.

10. Spencer Leeson, *Christian Education* (Longmans, Green & Co., Inc., 1947), pp. 21 ff. He also wrote *Christian Education Reviewed* (Longmans, Green & Co., Inc., 1957).

11. *Ibid.*, pp. 32 f.

12. *Ibid.*, p. 35.

13. *Ibid.*, p. 52.

14. Cf. Arthur Michael Ramsey, *An Era in Anglican Theology, from Gore to Temple* (Charles Scribner's Sons, 1960).

15. Leeson, *Christian Education*, p. 200.

16. M. V. C. Jeffreys, *Education: Christian or Pagan* (Educational Issues of Today, ed. by W. R. Niblett), (University of London Press, Ltd., 1946), p. 22.

17. *Ibid.*, p. 24.

18. *Ibid.*, Ch. V, pp. 68–90.

19. M. V. C. Jeffreys, *Glaucon: An Inquiry Into the Aims of Education*, (London: Sir Isaac Pitman & Sons, Ltd., 1950), p. v.

20. *Ibid.*, p. 167.

21. M. V. C. Jeffreys, *Beyond Neutrality: Five Essays on the Purpose of Education.* (London: Sir Isaac Pitman & Sons, Ltd., 1955).

10. A MEASURE OF THE MATTER

1. Cf. D. Campbell Wyckoff's discussion of the senior high objectives in *Theory and Design of Christian Education Curriculum.*

2. " Is Ecumenical Curriculum Possible? " See note 1 under " Preface."

3. Rachel Henderlite, *Forgiveness and Hope* (John Knox Press, 1961); *The Holy Spirit in Christian Education* (The Westminster Press, 1964).

4. Shinn, *The Educational Mission of Our Church.*

5. W. Kent Gilbert, *As Christians Teach* (Leadership Education Series, ed. by Philip R. Hoh) (Lutheran Church Press, 1962).

6. Gerard S. Sloyan, *Modern Catechetics: Method and Message in Religious Formation* (The Macmillan Company, 1963).

11. HISTORICAL DIMENSIONS FOR CHRISTIAN EDUCATION

1. *Basic Writings in Christian Education,* pp. 337 f.

2. For a fuller discussion of this point see Cully, *The Dynamics of Christian Education,* pp. 173 ff.

3. Lawrence Durrell, *Justine* (E. P. Dutton & Company, Inc., 1957).

4. Smart, *The Teaching Ministry of the Church,* p. 143.

5. Amos Wilder, *New Testament Faith for Today* (Harper & Row, Publishers, Inc., 1955), pp. 58 f.

6. R. G. Collingwood, *The Idea of History* (Oxford University Press; Galaxy Book, 1956), p. 248.

7. *Basic Writings in Christian Education,* p. 236.

8. *Ibid.,* p. 30.

9. *Ibid.,* p. 72.

10. Robert Ulich, ed., *Three Thousand Years of Educational Wisdom* (Harvard University Press, 1947).

11. This chapter is based in part on an article under the same title as the chapter published in *Religious Education,*

Vol. LIX, No. 5 (Sept.–Oct., 1964), pp. 378 ff., and is used by permission of the publisher, The Religious Education Association. This material also was presented in a public lecture under the Earl Foundation at the Pacific School of Religion during the 1961 summer session.

Index